LOVE, SEX, and RELATIONSHIPS

DEAN SHERMAN

LOVE, SEX, and RELATIONSHIPS

PUBLISHING

P.O. BOX 55787, SEATTLE, WA 98155

YWAM Publishing is the publishing ministry of Youth With A Mission. Youth With A Mission (YWAM) is an international missionary organization of Christians from many denominations dedicated to presenting Jesus Christ to this generation. To this end, YWAM has focused its efforts in three main areas: 1) Training and equipping believers for their part in fulfilling the Great Commission (Matthew 28:19). 2) Personal evangelism. 3) Mercy ministry (medical and relief work).

For a free catalog of books and materials write or call:

YWAM Publishing

P.O. Box 55787, Seattle, WA 98155

(425) 771-1153 or (800) 922-2143

Love, Sex, and Relationships
Copyright © 1999 by Dean Sherman

Published by Youth With A Mission Publishing
P.O. Box 55787
Seattle, WA 98155

Unless otherwise noted, Scripture quotations in this book are taken from the Holy Bible, New International Version®, Copyright© 1973, 1978, 1984 by the International Bible Society. Used by permission of Zondervan Publishing House.

Verses marked KJV are taken from the King James Version of the Bible.

ISBN 1-57658-141-1

Printed in the United States of America.

To my beautiful wife, Michelle, who has shown me depths and perspectives about love I never knew existed.

To Cherie and Troy, who are great father-trainers and so easy to love unconditionally.

THANK YOU, JIM DRAKE, FOR HELPING ME TO FINALLY GET THIS BOOK WRITTEN AND PUBLISHED.

Contents

Chapter One

WORLD, WE HAVE A PROBLEM

When I speak about relationships with the opposite sex, people often ask me why I choose this topic instead of something else. Two key events in my life convinced me that a frank, biblical discussion of love, sex, and relationships is vital for both the church and society.

Some years ago, I was in Wollongong, Australia, leading a street witnessing team. Late one evening, I had the opportunity to talk for an hour with a young man who seemed quite interested in the things of God. However, at the end of our conversation, he walked away not having made a commitment to Christ. After he left, I sat down on the sidewalk with my feet resting in the gutter to pray for this young Australian seeker.

After a few minutes, seven teenage girls tumbled out of a pub a few yards up the street from where I sat praying. Noticing this man sitting on the sidewalk, they came over and plopped down on either side of me. They had been drinking in the pub, so they felt at ease talking with me quite freely. During our conversation, they found out I was one of the Christians who had been witnessing up and down the street. They assured me that none of them could ever become a Christian because "Christians aren't allowed to have sex." As our discussion continued, they opened up further and began to share their personal sexual activity. Even though the oldest girl was only sixteen, each of them was regularly sexually active. What shocked me was that even with this degree of sexual activity none of the girls had an appreciation for sex or an understanding of how sex was designed to operate. They all expressed indifference toward marriage, reasoning that if the sex they experienced was all there was to marriage, then marriage was "no big deal."

At that moment, I got angry—not at the girls, but at the enemy who has ruined for untold thousands of people a wonderful gift God created for their fulfillment.

A few years later, I was speaking at a youth camp in the Gippsland area of Victoria in southern Australia. During my teaching time, on the third day of the camp, everyone left the auditorium for a tea break except one sixteen-year-old girl. She approached me and asked if she could speak with me. This young woman began our conversation by telling me she had had a baby the year before. "I was only fifteen," she said, "and I gave it up for adoption. It was very hard and traumatic for me, but that tough time is what brought me to the Lord."

As we talked, she continued to share her story: "I've been going to this church for about a year. There's a guy in the church that I really like. Last night he came to the window outside my dormitory, and I sneaked out with him. We went out into the trees and ended up having sex."

She began to cry, and her great fear spilled out. "Does this mean I'm not a Christian?"

"No," I replied. "That does not mean you are not a Christian."

"But I thought if I became a Christian, I wouldn't be able to do this," she sobbed.

I began to talk with her about human sexuality in light of the truth of Christianity. As people began to return from the break, our conversation came to a close. Before returning to her seat, she left me with a final bombshell.

"Most of the girls in the dormitory..." she began, "this is all they talk about."

I was hit with a powerful revelation. Many people do not understand what God thinks about human relationships and sexuality. I realized I did not love these young people if I did not address the subject that so often occupied their minds.

When the other students were seated, I shut my notebook and taught no more on the subject I had been speaking on. I opened the new session by stating that God is the one who thought up love, sex, and relationships. For the next three days, I had the rapt attention of every person in the auditorium.

OUR CULTURE IS PREOCCUPIED WITH ROMANTIC AND SEXUAL RELATIONSHIPS.

I teach on love, sex, and relationships because no single thing has had, is having, or will have as great an impact on any of our lives as romantic and sexual relationships.

Society knows this. The media play on the fact endlessly. Turn on the radio any time of the day or night and you will hear the same message in ninety percent of the songs. "I thought he loved me, but he left me." "I've never felt this way before, I know it's love." "How can I get her to see me in a crowded room?" It doesn't matter whether the song is heavy metal, pop, jazz, or country or whether it's sung in Spanish or English, the same message is being pushed: romantic and sexual love. Our whole culture is saturated with it. The majority of movies and television shows, books, and magazine articles are about love in some form. Teenagers rush home from school to watch TV soap operas, sitcoms, and talk shows. Will the fifteen-year-old student sleep with his English teacher? Will the woman tell her husband the baby she's carrying belongs to his brother? Will the daughter find out her mother is cheating on her father? The programs are different, but the plots are alarmingly similar. If you don't believe me, tune in to them sometime. Our culture is preoccupied with romantic and sexual relationships.

So I had to talk to those young people about relationships because they were preoccupied with the subject, and so was the culture in which we all lived. It's still that way today. Young people in the church are constantly being bombarded with messages about relationships that may or may not line up with God's truth.

I continue to talk about these issues because, believe it or not, we have a problem. You might say, "Speak for yourself. You might have a problem with this stuff, but not me; I've got it all together." But I repeat, we have a problem. The society we live in has a problem with relationships, and that problem affects every one of us.

The divorce rate in the United States is the highest in the world. Now, I'm not going to beat up on divorced people; in most cases they have already been beaten up on enough. I'm simply saying that it is a major problem. Today we have more sociology, more psychology, and more sex therapy than we've ever had before. We have more books, magazine articles, and seminars, and still people are divorcing at an incredible rate.

Adultery is also skyrocketing, even among missionaries and those involved in other ministries. What is adultery? It's the inability to relate properly to our neighbors. We don't love our neighbors, we just want to fulfill our desires with them. Adultery is an unloving act.

The rate of fornication (sex outside of marriage) is also a problem in our society. In high schools, fornication is not an isolated occasional occurrence; it is rampant. What is fornication? Fornication is an inability to relate properly to the opposite sex.

And what about lust? It has been estimated that ninety percent of all Western men and sixty percent of women have a problem with lust at some time in their life. What is lust? Again, it is the inability to relate properly to our neighbors. Instead of loving them, we are using them as the object of our fantasies.

As Christians, if we do not have a clear understanding of God's intentions in our relationships, we will go through our lives tossed and turned by society's every whim. Not only that, we will not be the light set on a hilltop that Jesus wants us to be. Christians have been given the answer to the world's relationship problems, and if we can grasp that understanding and impart it to others, we can do tremendous good to those around us. If we do not take the time to understand how God designed us to operate in relationships, we are not ready to live in society, and we are definitely not ready to minister to its needs.

This understanding of how God has designed us to operate in relationships is contained in a simple principle laid out for us in the Bible. In the next chapters we'll investigate this principle and then go on to look more closely at how it relates to our romantic and sexual relationships.

Chapter Two

THE BOTTOM LINE

What is God's basic principle for relationships? Jesus summed it up for us:

> Jesus replied: "Love the Lord your God with all your heart and with all your soul and with all your mind. This is the first and greatest commandment. And the second is like it: 'Love your neighbor as yourself.' All the Law and the Prophets hang on these two commandments." (Matthew 22:37–40)

This is a summary of the oldest message in the Bible. We are to love God with all our being and love our neighbors in the same way we love ourselves. God, others, ourselves, it's that simple. It's the bedrock of the gospel. If we do this one thing, everything else will fall into place.

While this is one of the oldest messages in the Bible, Jesus also reminds us in John 13:34, "A new commandment I give you: Love one another."

So the oldest message in the Bible is also the newest. Jesus has given us a new commandment. It is *the* commandment we are to live by.

This is the message you heard from the beginning: We should love one another. (1 John 3:11)

Dear friends, let us love one another, for love comes from God. Everyone who loves has been born of God and knows God. Whoever does not love does not know God, because God is love. (1 John 4:7–8)

There is no fear in love. But perfect love drives out fear, because fear has to do with punishment. The one who fears is not made perfect in love. We love because he first loved us. If anyone says, "I love God," yet hates his brother, he is a liar. For anyone who does not love his brother, whom he has seen, cannot love God, whom he has not seen. And he has given us this command: "Whosoever loves God must also love his brother." (1 John 4:18–21)

Let's think about this. Love is the message: loving God, loving others, loving ourselves. And what is love? Love is being in right relationship. I have spoken on relationships all over the world, from Thailand to Tanzania. Why? Because every sermon we've ever heard, every Bible verse we've ever read, every Christian workbook we've ever filled out, every seminar we've ever attended can be summed up like this: Love God, love your neighbor, love yourself.

RELATIONSHIP IS BASED ON VALUE.

Implicit in this love is value. Relationship is based on value. We relate to God first because He is the being in the universe with the most value. He is worth relating to, not because He is bigger than we are or because if we don't love Him we will go to hell. We relate to Him because He is worthy of our love.

We relate to Him through worship. We assign Him the "worth-ship" He deserves.

The second part of this commandment is that we are to love our neighbor as ourselves. Today we are not much different from the Pharisees who tried to trap Jesus by asking Him, "Who is my neighbor?" Of course, Jesus answered them with the parable of the Good Samaritan. The implication to the Pharisees, and to us, is that everyone is our neighbor. There are not some people who are in special categories where they no longer count as a neighbor. No, everyone, even the person we're romantically involved with, is our neighbor.

The Bible is very specific on this matter. It doesn't say love your neighbor instead of yourself, or love yourself instead of your neighbor; it says love your neighbor as yourself.

IT'S NOT MY TRUTH OR YOUR TRUTH THAT MATTERS; THERE IS ONLY ONE TRUTH, AND THAT IS GOD'S TRUTH.

If we love God but leave out loving our neighbor, we become mystics. Jesus told us we cannot love God and hate our brother. He connected the two. On the other hand, if we love our neighbor but leave out loving God, we are humanists. That's where we are in society today. Society tells us there is no objective truth, that all truth is relative to the situation. But Christianity says, It's not my truth or your truth that matters; there is only one truth, and that is God's truth.

Humanists have tried to turn the feeling of love itself into God. For them, God is love, and love is God. Love is the thread that runs through a happy relationship. Love is the force that watches over us as we play the lottery numbers. Love is the good vibes we get when we burn incense and discuss the meaning of life with our friends. But that simply isn't true. Love is not God. God is not a force or a flow or a good vibe. God is a being who is loving, kind, and compassionate. He is a being who wants to enjoy a relationship with each of us and who wants us to enjoy relationship with each other. In fact, He goes further than just wanting: He commands us to love Him, to love ourselves, and to love each other.

That is the bottom line of Christianity. Everything else is frills and extras. Without this reality burned into our soul, we are nothing and have nothing to say to the world or to each other. That may seem strong, but it's the bottom line. Don't just take my word for it, though. Listen to what Paul has to say about it:

> If I speak in the tongues of men and of angels, but have not love, I am only a resounding gong or a clanging cymbal. If I have the gift of prophecy and can fathom all mysteries and all knowledge, and if I have a faith that can move mountains, but have not love, I am nothing. If I give all I possess to the poor and surrender my body to the flames, but have not love, I gain nothing. (1 Corinthians 13:1–3)

So according to Paul, we can be a martyr, a brilliant theologian, even a miracle worker, but if we don't have love, we are nothing.

THE CHRISTIAN CHURCH HAS A TWO-THOUSAND-YEAR-OLD BAD HABIT OF NOT MAKING RELATIONSHIPS A TOP PRIORITY.

The reason I speak about relationship wherever I go is not that everyone needs a little talk about relationships or that it's less embarrassing to have a visiting speaker rather than the regular youth pastor talk about dating and sex. I choose to talk about relationships because simply put, if we don't get relationships right, we have very little left upon which to build our lives.

I suggest to you that every problem in the world is a problem of wrong relationship, where we are not loving God, others, and ourselves. And if that is the case, what does it say to us about relationships? It says relationships must become our top priority. If every problem in the world is a relationship problem and we don't relate well to just one person, then we are part of the problem. We might be a born-again, Bible-believing, Spirit-filled, miracle-working part of the problem, but we're part of the problem no less. I know that statement is direct and strong, but we need a wake-up call. The Christian church has a two-thousand-year-old bad habit of not making relationships a top priority. But God is clear in His Word. When we get along with each other, when we honor, serve, and embrace one another, we are, in fact, honoring and serving God. That's a powerful thought, one each of us should think about seriously.

Every time we relate in a right way to another human being, we are relating in a right way to God. Conversely, every time we relate in a wrong way to another human being, we are relating wrongly to God. Therefore, relationships must become our top priority. We must determine that even if we never do anything else, we are going to become good relators by the grace of God. If we never memorize another Bible verse, if we never sing in another gospel choir, if we never win another person to Jesus Christ, we are going to be a good relator. And if we don't do this, as Paul tells us, we will be loud clashing cymbals with lots of noise and hype, but nothing permanent to show for our efforts. Relationship is the most basic thing God asks of us. It is the bottom line.

By now you might be thinking, isn't witnessing important? Aren't we supposed to be out there witnessing for Jesus and winning lost souls into His kingdom? Of course we are. However, if relationship is the bottom line, I suggest our witnessing must be done through relationship. How does this square with what the Bible has to say? In John 13 Jesus tells His disciples: "All men

will know that you are my disciples if you love one another."
That's what witnessing is: convincing the world we are disciples
of the true Son of God.

PEOPLE WILL KNOW WE ARE REPRESENTATIVES OF THE LIVING GOD BY THE WAY WE LOVE AND RELATE TO EACH OTHER.

There are a lot of people in the world today, however, who
believe that there are no spiritual absolutes. They tell us they're
happy that Jesus works for us, but something else works equally
well for them. As long as we're happy, that's all that matters. We
might be a happy Buddhist, a happy Hindu, a happy heathen. It
doesn't matter which one we are, as long as we're happy. Don't
judge others for their belief in God, they tell us. Believing something, anything, is good for the soul. All the while we Christians
are jumping up and down and yelling, "No, no, no, you don't
understand. Our message is different. We really are the representatives of the Creator of the universe. We have a relationship
with Him through Jesus Christ." It gets frustrating sometimes trying to get this message across. How do we convince people that
not all religious roads lead to a holy and righteous God? Jesus
gave us the answer. It's so simple many of us gloss right over it.
People will know we are representatives of the living God by the
way we love and relate to each other.

Jesus constantly prayed while He was here on earth. Since
not many of His prayers are recorded, we have to believe that the
ones that are recorded have a special message for us. And what
do you think is the message in this prayer?

"My prayer is not for them alone. I pray also for those who
will believe in me through their message, that all of them may

be one, Father, just as you are in me and I am in you. May they also be in us so that the world may believe that you have sent me." (John 17:20–21)

A lot of people don't even believe Jesus existed. A lot of people who do believe He existed don't believe He rose from the dead or that His dying on the cross means anything more than that the Roman army finally caught up with Him and killed Him. And we are saying to them, "No, you don't understand. Jesus is God who became human to make a sacrifice as an atonement for sin. He is not just a prophet or a good man. Jesus is the only one who can take the burden of our sin and put it on Himself. He will come and live in us and change us from the inside out." It sounds crazy to the average nonbeliever! So how do we convince nonbelievers that it's true? We can try apologetics and logical arguments, but more than that, Jesus prayed and asked the Father to make us one so the world will be convinced of our message. When the world sees the way we relate to each other and the way we value each other and respect and honor each other, then the world will know two things: first, that we are God's representatives here on earth, and second, that the message of the gospel is true.

Down through church history we've tried just about everything else to win souls for Jesus. You've probably tried a bunch of them in your church or your missions group. But do you know what? We ought to try getting along. We ought to try appreciating and honoring each other! Now, doesn't that sound radical? We come up with all sorts of excuses for not doing it. We've gone so far as to burn each other at the stake in Jesus' name. Of course, today we don't burn each other at the stake anymore. It's not socially acceptable. So instead, we write books and magazine articles publicly criticizing each other. We slip snide remarks about each other into our conversations. We bring out our "prayer concerns" (read gossip) at church meetings to expose the weaknesses of our brothers and sisters. We don't want healing for them so much as we want vindication or justification for ourselves.

But none of these is a Christian activity. Period. The bottom line, according to Jesus, is that we love one another.

Right about now, many Christians start to panic. They think to themselves, Dean Sherman is in error; he seems to be advocating humanism. It sounds as if he is saying, "Let the truth and the Word of God go and just accept whatever someone wants to do." But why do so many Christians experience this gut reaction when told that the bottom line in the Christian faith is to love one another? It's because we have a dichotomy in our thinking. We think we have to be nice and love people, or we have to be firm and hold them to truth and righteousness. We think it's impossible to do both, that the two are opposites. But who is it that tells us to love one another? Jesus Himself. And who tells us not to compromise the truth? Jesus. So, if Jesus gave us both of these instructions, it must be possible to do them both.

So how is it possible to love other Christians but still be a bearer of God's truth in every situation? Paul gives us the answer:

> For by the grace given me I say to every one of you: Do not think of yourself more highly than you ought, but rather think of yourself with sober judgment, in accordance with the measure of faith God has given you." (Romans 12:3)

The greatest problem in relationships is thinking more highly of ourselves than we ought to think. If you have a problem in your family, it's because someone there is thinking more highly of himself or herself than he or she ought. If you have a problem in your marriage, someone in the marriage is thinking more highly of himself or herself than he or she ought. Is there a problem in your church? Guess what's at the root of it? Someone in your church is thinking more highly of himself or herself than he or she ought. What about problems in society? Does your community have a problem with race relationships? You guessed it. People from one race (or several races) are thinking of themselves more highly than they ought. Are there problems between men and women? It's the same thing. Someone is thinking of himself or herself more highly than he or she ought.

But can it really be this simple? Yes! Does the problem have a name? Yes. It's spelled P-R-I-D-E.

Pride, though, has two faces. One is superiority, and it's easy to recognize. Prideful people think they are better than others. "I pray more than you, and that makes me a better Christian." "We are the only move of God in this city. You have to do it like us or else," they say (but maybe not quite so bluntly!). It's not difficult to spot superior pride. Every hair on our body rises in protest when we are on the receiving end of it. But there is another form of pride, a more insidious form, because it mimics humility. Let me tell you how it works. People with this type of pride think more lowly of themselves than they ought. Inferior pride says, "I don't care. It doesn't matter. No one has ever cared about what I think, so why start now?" or, "I'm a worm. I've messed up my life. I'm going to marry the jerk because it's all I deserve."

This sounds humble at first, but it is actually pride. Why? Because it is not the truth. Pride involves moving outside of the truth about who we are, who others are, and who God is. True humility occurs when we move within that reality.

PRIDE INVOLVES MOVING OUTSIDE OF THE TRUTH ABOUT WHO WE ARE, WHO OTHERS ARE, AND WHO GOD IS. TRUE HUMILITY OCCURS WHEN WE MOVE WITHIN THAT REALITY.

Inferior pride is as much a barrier to relationship as superior pride. If we are not getting along with others, either they or us or both of us are moving in pride. And we know this for certain because when two people are functioning in true humility, it is impossible for them not to get along.

So what is the antidote for pride? It is to think with sober judgment in accordance with the measure of faith God has given us. But what is sober judgment? It is humility. It is having a correct assessment. It is recognizing who and what we really are. It is moving in the truth of who we are, who other people are, and who God is.

A proper relationship with any other person on this planet is really a matter of humility. We may not agree with everything the other person says, but we recognize that we are called to value, care for, and embrace that person. That is the basis of good relating.

Unity in any situation is simply relationship based upon humility. If we want unity in our marriage, both we and our spouse need to be moving in humility. Both of us must be willing to say "I'm sorry," willing to outdo each other in forgiveness, kindness, and servanthood. Unity is achieved the same way in our churches and youth groups.

"It can't be that simple," you protest. But it is. The problem is that most Christians don't see it because they are in despair. They are overwhelmed by the many problems around them and don't know where to start. There is only one starting point: having a right and honest estimation of ourselves and then moving in true humility. When we can do this, we will have the faith to minister to others and bring change to their lives as well.

But there is another problem that can hinder the way we relate to other people. Paul goes on in Romans to say:

> Just as each of us has one body with many members, and these members do not all have the same function, so in Christ we who are many form one body, and each member belongs to all the others. We have different gifts, according to the grace given us. (Romans 12:4–6)

A second significant problem we face in our relationships is our inability to appreciate differences and variety in others. We talk about people being weird and strange. Let me define *weird*. Weird is anybody significantly different from me! Any music that is different from the music I like is weird. Any way of dressing that is different from the way I dress is weird. Any worship that is not the way I choose to worship is weird. Are you getting the point? On the one hand, we are all inspired because God is the Creator of such abundant variety, yet on the other hand, we see as weird anything that is not exactly in line with the way we personally do things.

As if that's not enough, the devil comes along and helps us out. He whispers in our ear, "If you get too close to Jesus, you will lose your individuality. You won't have another creative thought. From here on you'll be conforming all the way. You get to follow the Christian rule book and nothing else." When we hear this, we start to think, "Yeah, Christians all walk the same, talk the same, and dress the same. If I identify with them, I will lose my uniqueness."

I don't know how many times I've heard people who were once serving God say, "I don't go to church anymore. I've had to go out on my own to find myself. In church everyone was pushing me into the mold. I needed to discover who I was." Usually I inquire, "And what are you doing now?" "Oh," they reply, "I'm living with my girlfriend (or boyfriend)." When I hear this, I nod my head and think: *Fornicating. Now that's unique. I haven't heard of that before. How creative can you get!*

The truth is, we cannot discover our uniqueness by sinning.

What if God were to give every Christian in the world a special twenty-four-hour dispensation to sin? And not just any sin, but the most creative, unique sin imaginable. When we reported back on what we had performed, we would find we had not performed a single unique sin that had not occurred in our grandparents' day in some form or other. There are no new ways to sin. Satan is not creative and unique. He is a copier and a counterfeiter.

We have been lied to. We cannot discover our uniqueness by sinning. It's been tried. Our anger, our lust, and our immorality look exactly like a hundred million other people's anger, lust, and immorality.

We cannot discover our uniqueness by doing selfish things. If we want to see uniqueness, we should check out God. Look at the variety in all He has made. Think of flowers. God could have said, "You want flowers? I'll give you flowers. Petunias, that ought to do you. You want colored flowers. Okay, you get pink flowers." God did not do that. Instead, He went all out. He gave us all kinds of flowers in all kinds of colors. He made butterflies and insects, amoebas and elephants. He created animals with stripes, dots, feathers, fur, tufts, and hair.

When it came to people, God did the same thing. He made an infinite range of temperaments and personalities. He made two sexes and gave us many different races. It didn't all happen as the result of some kind of genetic mutation. It came out of the mind of an all-wise God. It was an intentional part of His plan for mankind. He gave each race a gifting that other races will not share until they bow in humility and say, "You are a creation of God, and you have something to teach me."

God also made different giftings within the body of Christ, and He did so on purpose. He doesn't want us to have it all in our group. He wants us to reach out to one another and value what each has to offer and teach. We won't get anywhere in our relationships until we learn to appreciate the variety God has purposely put among us. Why try to change our spouse to be like us? Why have a pair of clones in a marriage? God wants us to appreciate the giftings He has given our spouse and complement them with our giftings.

As Christians, we believe relationships are necessary because people have value and our knowledge of value makes relationship necessary. What does this mean? Suppose I pull a small piece of paper out of my pocket. It's a rectangular piece of paper—that's all it is. It's printed on both sides, so it's not even much use to me. I drop the piece of paper on the floor and leave the room. A few minutes later the maid comes in to tidy the room. She has strict instructions to pick up any little pieces of paper and throw them into the fire. She sees the piece of paper I dropped on the floor and picks it up. Her eyes widen, and she looks around wondering what to do. Yes, it is a small piece of paper, and she was told to throw all small pieces of paper into the fire. But this little piece of paper is actually a 100-dollar bill. And knowing it is a 100-dollar bill, the maid cannot throw it into the fire. Against the orders of her boss, she stuffs it into her pocket.

"Ha!" we say. "That was not just a piece of printed paper, it was a 100-dollar bill that was dropped on the floor. That's different. No wonder the maid couldn't throw it away." But why is it different? It's different because the maid's knowledge of its value made it impossible for her to throw the piece of paper away. It had too much value to her.

Imagine you walked into what you thought was an empty room and found a tiny baby on the floor. Next to the baby was a huge cockroach. What would you do? If you were like most people, you would rush up to the baby and pick it up and at the same time stomp on the cockroach.

Think about it for a moment. You rescue the baby and kill the cockroach. But both of them were found abandoned in an otherwise empty room. What makes one worth rescuing and the other worth killing? This may sound like a trivial question, but it's not. At the heart of the answer is the reason why Christians are different from every other group on earth.

ORIGIN AND PURPOSE TOGETHER GIVE THINGS THEIR VALUE.

Think back to the 100-dollar bill. The bill had value for two reasons. First, its origin. It originated in a U.S. federal mint. If it had originated in someone's photocopier, it would have had no value. But it did not come from a copier; it originated in a mint. Next, it was designed for a purpose. The bill's purpose was to represent one hundred dollars in value within the United States. The presses at the federal mint could produce lovely pieces of green notepaper. The notepaper would have originated at the mint, but its purpose would have been to be not money but notepaper. It would not represent one hundred dollars in value. It is only the fact that the 100-dollar bill originated at the mint and that it was manufactured to be used as money that makes it valuable.

Origin and purpose together give things their value. Let's apply this principle to the cockroach and the baby.

Many worldviews agree, as do Christians, that God created everything. But some worldviews go a step further. They say that because God created all things, all things are of equal value to Him. They argue that all life is connected and no living thing has the right to take the life of another living thing.

These worldviews have erroneously equated origin with value. But origin is only half of the equation. Remember, value is the result of origin and purpose. This is why we can step on the cockroach without guilt. We do not have seminars called "Can a Christian Be a Pest Controller?" That would be ridiculous, because humans have a different purpose from cockroaches and killing one of them is not murder but the sensible thing to do to prevent disease. Not all religious worldviews can say that, though, because they have not added purpose into the equation of value. To them, anything God created has equal value in His sight.

A Christian is one who knows that God made human beings with a special purpose—the purpose of worshiping and fellowshiping with him. That purpose gives us infinitely more value than the cockroach.

Our knowledge of the origin and purpose of humans gives us an appreciation of their value, and that value makes it necessary for us to care for each other.

THE GOOD NEWS: RELATIONSHIP IS POSSIBLE

> But now in Christ Jesus you who once were far away have
> been brought near though the blood of Christ. (Ephesians 2:13)

Have you ever wondered how we can be far away from God when He is everywhere? How can we be far away from someone who is right beside us? But this verse from Ephesians is not talking about distance in feet or inches. It's talking about relationships. Have you ever been in a room with someone and thought to yourself, *There is a million miles between us?* In a physical sense, there isn't much distance between you at all, maybe only two feet; but we're not talking about physical distance, we're talking about a relationship barrier.

What did Jesus do on the cross? He died so that He could remove our sin. As a result, we who were sinners and far from Him in relationship could be brought near to Him. Now we can relate to God because Jesus has closed the gap for us.

> For he himself is our peace, who has made the two one and
> has destroyed the barrier, the dividing wall of hostility, by

abolishing in his flesh the law with its commandments and regulations. His purpose was to create in himself one new man out of the two, thus making peace, and in this one body to reconcile both of them to God through the cross, by which he put to death their hostility. (Ephesians 2:14–16)

JESUS DIED TO REMOVE THE RELATIONSHIP BARRIER BETWEEN US.

Jesus Christ bled and died to remove enmity so that we could relate to others. I can now relate to you, and you can relate to me regardless of our different gender, race, or nationality because Jesus died to remove the relationship barrier between us.

Once I was dead to Christ, but now I am alive to Him. I used to be lost in my sin, but Jesus took my sin away and put it upon Himself. That is why I can say I am related to God, and I can relate to others because Jesus removed the enmity. This is referred to as being saved by grace. Grace is giving someone what he or she doesn't deserve. In the same way, we can relate to others by grace. We can give the other person something he or she doesn't deserve, based on the fact that Jesus has died and taken away the enmity between us.

Through the death and resurrection of Jesus I can relate to God and I can relate to others. I can even relate properly to myself. It's only then that I can fulfill God's ultimate purpose for me: to love Him and to love my neighbor as myself.

In the next chapter we will discuss relationships with the opposite sex, which may be the reason you picked up this book in the first place. But as you read on, do not forget the groundwork we have laid in this chapter. The reason I have focused on general relationships here rather than on specific ones is that there is no relationship in the world that should fall outside the orb of loving God first and then loving our neighbor as ourselves, because there is no one who does not qualify as our neighbor. Entering into a romantic relationship with another person does not remove that person from the designation of being our neighbor. So we can see that every relationship a Christian is involved in has the same parameters—loving the other person in the same way we would want to be loved and valuing the person as one who is created by God for the purpose of relationship with Him.

Chapter Three

BACK TO THE BEGINNING

> In the beginning God created the heavens and the earth. Now the earth was formless and empty, darkness was over the surface of the deep, and the Spirit of God was hovering over the waters. (Genesis 1:1)

Here, in the very first verse of the Bible, we learn that God created the universe. First He makes stars and constellations, then mountains and oceans. These aren't copies of things that have existed before; they are original creations thought up in the mind of God. What creativity! And after He has fashioned the mountains and oceans, God decides to make living things. He makes plants, trees, ferns, mushrooms, and grasses. He invents pollen and seeds, roots and leaves. Then He moves on to animal life. Here I think God had a lot of fun. If you don't think God has a sense of humor, visit a zoo sometime. You'll see animals with long necks, animals with no necks, animals with one horn and others with two horns, not to mention some animals that have a whole row of horns down their back. Each of these living creatures was an original thought up and created by God. And not only did God bring every living creature into being, but these creatures interrelated perfectly with all the other things He had made. The animals would eat the plants, the seeds of these plants would be carried by the animal and deposited far away, where they would begin to grow. It all worked perfectly. God took care of all the intricate details to make it happen.

Even with all of this plant and animal life, the Bible tells us that God was not satisfied. There was one more thing He wanted to create.

> Then God said, "Let us make man in our image, in our likeness." (Genesis 1:26)

None of us can fathom all that these words mean. What we can draw from them is that something about what we are on the outside as well as on the inside bears the stamp of the likeness of God.

Once God had decided to make something in His own image, He reached down to the dirt and began to fashion a human being. He created the head with hair, ears, eyes, a nose, and a mouth. Did you know there are over one million working parts in your eye alone? God is a careful and precise creator. He thought through all the little details in relation to every other part of our body. He gave us taste buds. Now what could we possibly need taste buds for? For pleasure? And what about our erogenous zones? Why would God make some areas in our body very sensitive to touch? Were they created for pleasure, too?

Reading this, some of you are ready to put the book down! *Hold it a minute*, you're thinking, *isn't pleasure from the devil? If we get pleasure from our erogenous zones, either they kicked in after the fall, or God made a mistake!* I don't believe God made a mistake, and I certainly don't think our erogenous zones are a result of the fall. God is an extravagant God. God understands pleasure and designed human beings to experience it. Some of us have a difficult time believing this. It doesn't sound at all like the austere, killjoy God we may have been taught about in Sunday school. I was taught this way, but then I discovered that the Bible tells us differently.

> You have made known to me the path of life; you will fill
> me with joy in your presence, with eternal pleasures at your
> right hand. (Psalm 16:11)

Do we really believe that in God's right hand He has pleasures for us? Pleasure is something very dear to the heart of God,
something He deliberately programmed into human beings.

Sexual relations bring pleasure. Many Christians are shocked
to hear a preacher say that. But why? God thought of such pleasure and brought it into being. Yet as Christians we often think
of sexual things as not quite holy or pure. We tend to think that
if we just get close enough to God we won't have to think about
it. But how can thinking about sex be "dirty" or "unholy" when
sex and sexual pleasure themselves were conceived in the mind
of a pure and holy God? God is incapable of a dirty or unholy
thought.

In Genesis 2:18, after He has created man, God says to
Himself, "It is not good for the man to be alone." The word *good*
here is not a very accurate translation. The word in the original
text is meant to carry the idea of not being complete. So God is
really saying here, "What I envisaged is not quite finished yet.
Something is missing." So He put the man to sleep and took
something out of him with which He could fashion another
being that was very similar. He used a part of the man to make a
woman. By doing so, God showed that the two would always be
linked together as a part of each other. We often talk about the
"opposite" sex, but God did not intend for us to see ourselves as
opposite or opposing each other. We were not created to be com-
petitive; we were designed to complete each other. We were created to work in tandem.

In acknowledging that God created men and women, we
must also acknowledge that He is the creator of our sexuality.
But even knowing this is true is too much for many Christians to
face. As a result, in the church we have come to see the female
body as an evil thing and a cause of lust and sin. How many
times in how many churches has the following scenario played
itself out? The youth pastor gets up and says, "Okay, kids, we're
going on an outing to the lake (or river or swimming pool). Now

I want to talk to you girls. You know what is acceptable to wear. You know that certain clothes are going to cause your brothers to sin…"

Will someone tell me what type of clothes forces a man to lust? We find it hard to come up with an answer. Why? Because no type of clothing causes lust. Lust is not caused. Men lust after women who wear ankle-length skirts and blouses that button all the way to their chins. Men lust when women wear long robes and have every part of their body covered except for a narrow slit to see through. Men even lust when they withdraw themselves into monasteries and do not see a woman for twenty years! Lust is in the mind of the man, and it is a lie to say that women cause it. It is possible to observe the human body and not lust.

The girls in the youth group have every right to stand up and say to their youth pastor, "Hold it, I didn't buy this body at Walmart; this is the way I was created. This body was fashioned by a pure and holy God. My body is not the reason a brother sins."

CHRISTIANS MUST STOP MAKING DIVISIONS BETWEEN HOLY LIVING AND SEXUALITY.

No one's body has ever caused another person to sin. The sin comes from within the sinner, not from the body the sinner looked at. Jesus made it clear that it's not what goes into people that defiles them but what comes out. There is nothing on earth we can look at that will cause us to have to sin. Sin comes from within. Let me illustrate. Two men can look at the same picture of a woman's breasts. One man commits the sin of lust as he looks at the picture, while the other man, a surgeon, who instead studies the picture to work out where he will make a life-saving incision, does not. Both men were looking at the same photo, but they did not both lust after the woman.

Christians must stop making divisions between holy living and sexuality. God intended the two to exist together in the Christian church, yet somehow we have divided them, and that division has become widespread.

What about the Garden of Eden? God came down and walked and talked with Adam and Eve, a naked couple with their hormones and sexuality fully functioning. He smiled when He saw them and said, "This is very good." Yet we portray sexuality as some kind of mistake, some kind of flaw that we had better try to help God cover up. But we couldn't be more mistaken.

What God has pronounced to be very good we ought not ever call evil or wicked. I've heard Christian men describe their wives like this, "She's an angel in public, but she's a demon in the bedroom," nod, nod, wink, wink. Or, "I'm in luck, I think my wife is feeling a little wicked tonight."

What an insult such remarks are to God. Can we see the perversion that has slipped into such comments? We think that abandoned, adventurous sexuality is Satan's realm. Again we couldn't be more mistaken.

What is the biggest hoax of all time? It is when the devil comes to us and says, "I'm the sex expert. If you get too goody-goody, too holy and pure, you're going to miss some exciting thrills and chills when it comes to sex." And when he whispers this to us, all too often we fall for it. I hear it over and over again when I counsel young Christian men. They say to me, "I know I'm supposed to settle down someday to a pure Christian girl, but in the meantime I feel like I'm missing out. I wouldn't mind getting some experience and finding out a few things. What's wrong with a little experimenting? It doesn't really hurt anyone, does it?"

I hear girls say, "My mother insists I can date or marry only a Christian guy, but most of the Christian guys I meet are lame. They're just not with it, if you know what I mean." I do know what they mean! They mean their idea of a real man is someone who is not submitted to God. They mean real men are "a little wicked." We destroy ourselves in our young years because we believe Satan's lie that he is a sex expert and has the scoop on sexual pleasure.

How can I be sure the devil is lying? It's very easy, really. Satan is an angel, and angels are not sexual beings. Angels are neutered, like your cat or dog is after you take it to the vet. Satan does not have one ounce of sexual experience or sexual ability. Now, Genesis chapter six tells us there was a brief time in history when angels did have sexual relations, but not with each other. When they wanted to have sex, they came to human beings, because we're the ones God created to have sex, not angels. Jesus said, "The thief comes only to steal and kill and destroy, I have come that you may have life, and have it to the full" (John 10:10). Can it be any clearer than this? Every time we make a choice to follow God's way in sexual relationships, we make Satan angry. Satan has failed in his mission once again. Every act of submission to God and choosing to follow His ways mocks Satan. The devil has never desired sexual fulfillment for anyone; his only intention is to bind and destroy us.

Millions of people, including Christians, are bound by sex. They think about it all the time. They are driven by it and spend their money seeking sexual fulfillment. They do not control their sexual desires; their sexual desires control them. The devil is leading them around by the nose. He has drawn them into bondage.

Some of the saddest people I talk to are teenagers who have so messed with God's plan for sexual fulfillment and pleasure that they are already burned out on sex. They are sixteen or seventeen years old, and already sex has caused them so many heartaches and problems that they don't want anything more to do with it. It doesn't excite them one bit anymore. Instead; it makes them feel used and tired. When I talk to young people like this, I get angry at what they've allowed the devil to do to them.

When we want to find out the best way to handle our sexuality, we shouldn't listen to the devil's lies. Instead we must go back to God and inquire of Him. After all, sex was His idea, and He knows exactly how to lead us to the most fulfilling, satisfying, abundant life.

If I buy a new car, I don't want a manual from a refrigerator company. If I want to get peak performance from my car, I need the manufacturer's manual for that car, not one for an appliance.

Likewise, if I want to get the most fulfillment out of my relationships, including male/female ones, I need to get as close as possible to the one who thought up the whole process—God!

We need to understand that we will be missing out on God's highest if we do not relate to others in the way we were created to do so. Satan has no wish and no ability to lead us into sexual fulfillment. Period. We must stop listening to him. We must go on the offensive.

YOU CANNOT BE TOTALLY WHOLE IN YOUR PERSONALITY UNLESS YOU ARE WHOLE IN JESUS CHRIST.

Who are the people in this world who are the most sexually fulfilled in themselves and are the most sexually fulfilling to their partners? They are the people who are most whole in Jesus Christ. Now I don't mean all Christians here. You can be born again and heaven bound and not be whole in your personality. You cannot be totally whole in your personality unless you are whole in Jesus Christ, body, soul, mind, emotions, and spirit.

In contrast to this, look at those the world tells us have it together in the area of relationships. Athletes, movie stars, models, the very ones who are jumping from bed to bed to bed, and relationship to relationship. Who is Satan trying to fool here?

Christians should be the sex experts on Earth. After all, our God thought sex up. So as followers of Jesus Christ, who better than you and I to be the ones the world comes to for answers about sex and relationships. We just better be sure that when people come to us we have God's answers to share with them. As you read on, you will begin to see what God's answers are.

⌁ Chapter Four

TWISTED TRUTHS

*I*f we were to go into a kindergarten class and ask the boys to line up on one side of the room and the girls on the other, we wouldn't see a group of confused children in the middle wondering which side of the room they should line up on. At age five, boys know they are boys and girls know they are girls. But that's not the way things are for adults in our society. An increasing number of people are struggling with their sexual and gender identity.

Another obstacle to healthy relationships faced by many is that of feeling inferior. A large amount of what we do in life is governed by how we feel about ourselves deep within. Many people who abuse their bodies with alcohol, drugs, or illicit sex know these things are self-destructive, but are driven to do them because they feel inferior. They feel inferior because society has told them they're not all they are supposed to be. They are the wrong color, they have the wrong sized body parts, they come from the wrong part of town. When people accept these false messages, depression and a sense of inadequacy often set in.

These two problems—confusion over sexual identity and inferiority—are fed by two "twisted" truths. I call them twisted truths because the basis of them is true, but the devil puts a twist on them and then fires them at us. What are these two twisted truths?

WE ARE ALL UNIQUE. THERE IS ONLY ONE OF ME AND ONE OF YOU IN ALL THE WORLD.

First, the devil whispers to us that we are different and that being different means there is something wrong with us. The truth here is that we are all unique. There is only one of me and one of you in all the world. When I was growing up, it was known that everyone had a unique fingerprint. Since that time we have learned that a lot more than our fingerprints are unique. Our brainwaves are unique, our voice pattern is unique, the pattern in the cornea of our eye is unique, the DNA on every strand of our hair is unique, even the shape of our ears is unique. God went all out when He created us. There is not one thing about us that is mass-produced.

Why are women willing to pay thousands of dollars for a dress from Saks Fifth Avenue and other boutiques? It's because they know they are buying a designer original. That means there is only one dress like it in the whole world. No matter what ball or gala they go to, they know that no one else will be wearing a dress identical to theirs. Likewise, God has made each of the over six billion human beings on earth today designer originals. No matter where we look or for how long, we will never find another person identical to us. That's amazing. God didn't use an assembly line. We might have done it that way and produced people in batches, but not the endlessly creative God. He delights in making each of us a designer original.

Yet it is the fact that no two of us are alike that the devil uses to trip so many of us up. Now, perhaps more than at any other time, people are confused about their gender. We must not allow models and ideas of masculine or feminine behavior within a culture to affect our confidence about who we are. Satan is having a field day using social type casting to confuse us with gender stereotypes. So it's time we learn the truth about ourselves.

(1) *Everyone is different.* If you are a man, you may not share the same interests of other men. So what? Maybe you think all other men like to watch sports and you do not, or that all men love to get grease and oil under their fingernails while you desire a manicure.

Or if you're a woman, maybe you never enjoyed playing with dolls or wearing lacy clothes. Maybe you are not what our culture would define as a typical (i.e., feminine) girl and you would rather drive a gravel truck. That doesn't mean there is anything wrong with you. You are a unique expression of an endlessly creative God.

(2) *Each person must accept himself or herself as he or she is.* So be honest and accept the fact you are not like other men or women. Jesus said the truth will set you free, so it's okay to stop pretending you enjoy things you really think are boring or are bored by things you really enjoy.

Some homosexuals say, "I can trace it back to very early in my life; therefore it must be true." But that doesn't necessarily follow. I can remember very early in my life feeling like I was the odd one out because I wore glasses and was very skinny. I felt as though I wasn't like everyone else, that I never fit in. This is a very distinct memory from early in my life, but does that make it a truth I should carry with me the rest of my life? No. I may have started thinking those things at a very early age, but that does not make them the truth. Satan is expert at lying to us. Even at a very early age he whispers to us, "You're not acceptable. You're too fat (or skinny), your hair is red, it's thick and curly." And if he can convince us we are not a real man or a real woman, he will then attempt to sow the same kind of doubts in our minds about our gender orientation.

Whenever we accept some or all of the devil's lie, we conform ourselves to that lie. It doesn't matter whether it has to do with sexual orientation or poor self-image. We must be careful not to accept what is not the truth.

HOW DO WE DETERMINE WHAT IS THE
TRUTH? THERE ARE ONLY TWO WAYS.
EITHER WE FOLLOW THE TRUTH GOD
HAS ESTABLISHED, OR WE MAKE "TRUTH"
UP FOR OURSELVES AS WE GO ALONG.

How do we determine what is the truth? There are only two ways. Either we follow the truth God has established, or we make "truth" up for ourselves as we go along. The biblical worldview says that God is the purveyor of truth, while the humanist view says that everything is relative. According to this view, our truth changes depending on time and location. When we go along with this view, we open ourselves up to accepting whatever junk Satan wants to load on us. For example, we accept social type-casting as truth. What does this mean? It means that we accept whatever society says is the "correct" way to be, as if it were absolute truth instead of social convention. Society might say, for instance, that if a man wears deodorant, he is showing a lack of masculinity. In fact, the society might dictate that men should not wear any scent—not only no deodorant but also no after-shave or scented soap. Most American men would scoff at this today, but did you know that in 1946 there was only one brand of men's deodorant on sale in the United States? Even selling that one brand was a retailing gamble. The whole idea that a man should smell good is a recent phenomenon. The accepted norms of a society change with area and era.

I was raised in Idaho, where the main industries were manly pursuits like logging, mining, and farming. From there I moved around. During the 1980s, I lived in Hawaii. While there I became partial to wearing white pants and flowery shirts. Pink and purple shades were my favorite colors for these shirts. To top it off, when I went to formal events, I was often presented with a huge garland of flowers that I wore as a necklace. If I had gone back to my high school in Idaho wearing my Hawaiian garb, I might have been beaten up before I got out of the parking lot for not dressing "like a man." You see, what is acceptable as masculine and feminine is very relative, depending on where you are, at what time, and with whom.

When I was a teenager, the girls were trying desperately to look like Marilyn Monroe—the epitome of an acceptable female. No matter that the girls had to stuff their bras and wear belts around their waist that almost cut off their circulation. Then in the 1960s, the model Twiggy hit the scene. Suddenly all the stuffing came out of the bras as girls began seeing how flat-chested they could make themselves look. They wanted to be so thin you would mistake them for a broomstick. Many girls couldn't look like that without completely messing up their minds and bodies with anorexia or bulimia. These illnesses became a serious problem as millions of young girls took their cue from a society that said to be really cute and feminine you had to be obsessively skinny.

TODAY, MORE THAN AT ANY OTHER TIME IN HISTORY, WE ARE BEING DELUGED WITH MEDIA IMAGES THAT "HELP" US TO DEFINE WHAT IS SUPPOSEDLY MASCULINE AND FEMININE.

I hope we're all beginning to see the dangers of conforming ourselves to human stereotyping instead of God's truth. It's an insidious temptation. Today, more than at any other time in history, we are being deluged with media images that "help" us to define what is supposedly masculine and feminine. No wonder we're in such a mess!

When we watch TV, we hear men say things like, "I was with a real woman tonight, and believe me, she was a whole lot of woman." What effect does this have on the women watching?

They begin to ask themselves, "If I don't look like that woman, can I be a real woman?" Or a woman on a TV show says, "I was with a *real* man last night." Deep down the men ask themselves, "Am I a *real* man? Do I have what it takes?"

Satan is happy to use the media or any other means to get his message across. And what is his message? It is that we are not acceptable the way God made us. As a result, people are drowning themselves in alcohol, other drugs, sex, and alternative lifestyles, either to escape or to build false confidence.

This mistake of looking to anyone other than God to confirm our gender and make us feel included has produced deep wounding in the hearts of thousands of young boys. These boys have been made to feel that because they don't like to do many "manly" things, they are not real men. Out of hurt and bitterness and the knowledge that they cannot or do not want to be like the stereotype, they have sealed off parts of themselves. Their hurt has caused them to reject something as basic as their own sexuality. Here again we must go back to the mind of God and ask Him what He conceived and created. What exactly does He consider a real man or a real woman?

The answer is simple and straightforward. This is how you find out whether you are one hundred percent real woman or real man. If you're a female, you are one hundred percent real woman. It can't be that easy, you say. But it is. If you're a female, you are as much a woman as anyone who ever lived. It doesn't matter if you don't like frilly things. It doesn't matter if you drive an eighteen wheeler. It doesn't matter what your body size is. None of these things matter because they have nothing to do with whether you are a woman or not. Period.

Likewise, if you're a male, you are one hundred percent real man. You are as much a man as any man who has walked the earth. It doesn't matter whether or not you like contact sports or rebuilding your car just for the fun of it. It doesn't matter whether you have a hairy chest or are totally hairless!

To use any other standard to judge ourselves by is to fall into the trap of comparing ourselves with other people.

God created two sexes and we are either one sex or the other. One hundred percent. We are not sixty percent one and forty percent the other. We're not even ninety-nine percent one and one percent the other. We are either fully male or fully female.

But what about people who claim God made them another way? And what about the brain and the strange chromosome? It is a fact that people have a wide variety of physiological and emotional makeups. Some would therefore argue that this allows them to function sexually and romantically in a way God clearly never intended. The good news is that nothing you are physically or emotionally causes you to have to violate God's truth. Nothing!

And the truth is, God designed you. To get out of the confusion and hurt you may be feeling about your gender identity, you have to keep reminding yourself of God's truth rather than society's stereotypes. Remember, almost everybody struggles either with gender identity or inferiority. We all need God's redemptive power to make us new creatures, and we all need the constant renewal of our minds from His Word so that we are conformed to the truth and not the lie. Through the renewal of your mind, you can be healed and walk in self-confidence. You will be able to look at yourself in the mirror and say, "Thank You, God, for the way You thought up and designed me. It is very good."

♪ Chapter Five

THE GIFT OF ATTRACTION

Once I was running a Bible training school, and a young man in the school came up to me and said, "Dean, I want to tell you up front that before I became a Christian I was a real womanizer. I was involved in all sorts of immorality, and I want you to know that while I'm in this school I am not going to have anything to do with women."

"Okay," I said.

During the school I noticed he was spending quite a lot of time with a particular young woman, and when he noticed that I noticed, he came and spoke with me again. "You will have noticed I've been spending a lot of time with Sue. I want you to know there is no attraction. It's all in the Lord," he said.

Notice the implication in what he said. Either his relationship with Sue is in the flesh, in which case attraction is involved, or it's in the Lord and there's no attraction.

Young men come up to me all the time and say, "Would you pray for me? I think I have a demon." I ask them what makes them think that, and they usually say, "Because I like women, and no matter how hard I try not to do so, I still do. I think I might have a demon or something." Indeed, it's not only males who say this to me; many females feel the same way over young men.

NOT ONLY DID GOD MAKE TWO SEXES, BUT HE MADE THE TWO SEXES TO BE ATTRACTED TO EACH OTHER.

I then have to tell them I can't cast a demon out of them because there is nothing to cast out! The feelings they're experiencing are feelings God gave them. It's not their lower nature or their old self asserting itself. It's something God created welling up within them. You see, not only did God make two sexes, but He made the two sexes to be attracted to each other. The ability to be attracted to another person is a gift of God.

Some of us find this fact hard to believe because attraction is the point where we begin to run into problems. If it weren't for attraction, we tell ourselves, we would not have problems with lust and adultery.

It's not surprising, then, that a number of theologians down through church history have taught that all attraction is of the flesh. They contend that even in marriage people should have sex only to make babies and for no other reason. But their reasoning is a twisting of the truth and a rejection of a gift of God.

So what about this gift of attraction God has given us? What is it, and how do we use it appropriately?

Have you ever watched a baby discover it has hands? When we were born, we had no idea we had hands. Our hands were totally out of our control. Indeed, our mother may have put cotton mittens on our hands to stop us from scratching ourselves with our fingernails or poking ourselves in the eye! But as time went by, we began to notice that the things at the end of our arms were connected. We began to figure out that with a lot of practice we could make the hands do things for us. It is a wonderful thing to watch this self-discovery take place in a baby.

So it is with the mechanism inside us called attraction. The problem is that most people have not figured out that they have an attraction gift just as surely as they have hands. Or if they have, they don't know how to use it the way God intended it to be used. They are like babies who have realized they have hands but have no clue how to make them work. Just as babies need to know how to use their hands properly if they are to grow up and enjoy a normal life, we need to understand our attraction gift. Do you love a sunset? Do you enjoy the tranquility of mountains and lakes and carpets of wildflowers? What about food? Do some things smell so delicious that you can't wait until lunch? Are you attracted to beautiful music, classical art, or modern poetry?

YOUR ATTRACTION GIFT IS AS UNIQUE AS YOUR THUMBPRINT.

The things we are attracted to have to do with our personality. So does that make attraction of the flesh? Should it be suppressed? Not at all. Attraction to food, art, beautiful sunsets, or music is a functioning mechanism God has gifted all human beings with. He has not gifted animals with such an attraction gift. Horses and cows are not attracted to a spectacular sunset. We do not see dogs and pigs visiting art galleries. Why? Because animals are regulated by instinct, and appreciating a sunset or art in a gallery is not one of these instincts. Humans, on the other hand, have had a unique gift placed within them. This attraction gift is not a sin, nor is it of the flesh, nor is it a demon. Rather, it is a very special gift of God to those who are made in His image. We are not only animals. We are not driven by chemical reactions within to do the things we do. We are creatures to whom God has given a special gift, the gift of free choice. We have a sense of right and wrong placed within to guide our actions.

Once a baby knows it has hands, it has to find out how to properly use them. So let's take a closer look at this attraction gift so that rather than fear it, we can learn to enjoy it and reap its benefits. The attraction gift has several features.

THE ATTRACTION GIFT IS UNIQUE

Your attraction gift is as unique as your thumbprint. People are not all attracted to the same car or the same hairstyle or the same furniture. Nor are they all attracted to the same people.

Have you ever heard the hype about your friend's new boyfriend or girlfriend and then finally met the person? What does your friend see in him or her, you wonder. The new boyfriend or girlfriend is nothing like the wonderful person described to you. The truth is, you're just not seeing the person the same way your friend is. Your friend is attracted to the person, and you are not. This is a good thing. If we were all attracted to the same people, there would be millions of lonely people around whom nobody was attracted to, while a few very popular people would be spending all their lives fending off others! But God has made us all unique and different and has given us different and unique attraction gifts.

With regard to uniqueness, we need to get one thing straight. We must not mistake character weakness for uniqueness. While God has made us with a unique attraction gift, He expects us to develop our character. It is not a form of uniqueness to fornicate. My uniqueness does not allow me to steal or to have a bad temper. That is character weakness, and Jesus died to remove our character weaknesses and take away our sins. He did not die to take away our uniqueness.

GOD DESIGNED US TO HAVE VERY
CLOSE FRIENDS OF THE SAME SEX
AS WELL AS THE OPPOSITE SEX.

THE ATTRACTION GIFT CAN FUNCTION TOWARDS MEMBERS OF THE SAME SEX

To many this is a surprising thought. It shouldn't be. God designed us to have very close friends of the same sex as well as the opposite sex. Some of my deepest, most affectionate friendships are with men. Am I a homosexual? No. Am I in danger of becoming one? No. That is not a proud boast but an accurate understanding of how God has made me and the attraction gift within. God set me up to be attracted to the same sex, and He has made all of us the same way. My God-given attraction to my same sex can be deeply enjoyed without assuming sexual or romantic possibilities. Society today has become so confused on this point that it has made people who have deep same-sex relationships feel as though they are on the verge of becoming something other than what God made. This is not the case, and such confusion has robbed many people of both sexes from the fulfilling relationships God had planned for them.

THE ATTRACTION GIFT WORKS TOWARDS THE OPPOSITE SEX

How many of us have wondered whether there is something deficient about our Christianity because we have been attracted to the opposite sex? It's amazing how many Christian young people think something is wrong with them. They wish their attraction gift would dry up and go away! They think that if they can get to a high enough spiritual plateau they will not be attracted to the opposite sex. That's simply not true, and it is never going to happen. God has made the opposite sex attractive to us, and He has made us attractive to the opposite sex. That is the way things are always going to be.

Many Christians believe that admitting to being attracted to the opposite sex is tantamount to setting themselves up to sin. But that is twisted thinking. It's like saying that if I admit I have a hand, I'll end up hitting you with it. To think this way is fatalistic and absurd.

When I was growing up, we had a lot of visiting ministries come through our church. Usually, they consisted of a preacher and his wife, who would play the piano. Somewhere in the course of his message, the preacher would look over at his wife and say something like, "Since I met my wonderful wife here, no other woman in the world is attractive to me." He would say this to emphasize his fidelity and spirituality. But was it accurate or necessary to say? I think his righteous living may have been coexisting with a misunderstanding of how we are actually made. God has made us to be attractive to others and to be attracted by them. And this gift does not stop when we start wearing a wedding ring.

The gift of attraction does not lead directly to a violation of truth. When I say to an audience, "I like women," some people begin to look panicked. I can see it on their faces. They're thinking, "What does he mean? Is he about to confess something? He sure sounds on dangerous ground."

Why do people react like this? Why do they think there is a direct causal link between attraction and sin? Consider this. Imagine I were to go out into the parking lot after church to see your new car. I say to you, "I really like your car. I've always wanted a car just like that. I like the shade of red. I like the sunroof. I like the legroom. I like the upholstery. It's a great car." Do you say to yourself, "Quickly, lock the car. Dean Sherman likes it. I won't take it near his house in case he finds a way to steal it." Such a response wouldn't enter your mind. My attraction to your car is in no way linked to my stealing your car.

Are you getting the point? Attraction does not equate to sin. If the car was stolen, you wouldn't automatically assume I stole it. Your knowledge of my character would tell you I do not steal.

Neither should we conclude that attraction to the same sex or the opposite sex is connected in any way to a violation of truth, be it homosexuality or adultery. We need to understand that our attraction gift can work apart from violations of truth. Violations of truth equate to attraction plus character weakness, not just attraction.

The bottom line is that God has gifted us and created us to be attracted to the opposite sex. Some of my deepest affectionate friendships are with women. These women are my friends. Is that all right? Yes. Am I an adulterer? No. My attraction does not have to lead to adultery.

Neither does our attraction gift mean God wants us to sin. This is where some Christians have things the wrong way around. They say, "Because God made me attracted to someone (whichever sex it might be), He must think it's okay to follow through and have sex with them." This reasoning is contrary to what God had in mind when He gave us an attraction gift. Not making this assumption will help us control our natural gifting and use it righteously. That way, we don't have to either deny we have attraction or let it excuse wrong behavior.

THE GIFT OF ATTRACTION OPERATES TOWARDS ANOTHER PERSON'S PHYSICAL FEATURES

What this means is that when we meet someone, we can be either attracted or not attracted to the person's physical features, such as the shape of the body, color of the eyes, and smell of the hair.

Right about now some readers will be thinking, "Hold on a minute. I don't need to be reading this in a Christian book. I'm trying to be holy and forget all about worldly stuff. If we're good Christians, we shouldn't even be thinking about another person's physical features. After all, the closer a person gets to Jesus, the less we notice what the person looks like on the outside. God looks at the heart, the inside of a person, and that's what we should be concentrating on, too."

Many Christians think this way. By sheer will power they can ignore the attraction to the physical features of others for short bursts of time. But then one morning, one of these "heavenly minded" Christians is reading and praying, trying to concentrate solely on the Holy Word of God, and what does this person read? "When Abram came to Egypt, the Egyptians saw that she [Sarah] was a very beautiful woman. And when Pharaoh's officials saw her, they praised her to Pharaoh" (Genesis 12:14–15). Or "He [David] was ruddy, with a fine appearance and handsome features" (1 Samuel 16:12). "Not fair," these heavenly minded Christians declare. "I'm trying not to think about these things, and now I have a picture of Sarah in my head. She's good-looking and has a great body, and I see David with strong muscles and deep brown eyes. He has flashing white teeth, and he's smiling at me."

Now our heavenly minded Christians are confused. They feel uncomfortable thinking about biblical characters being beautiful or attractive. Indeed, they wonder whether they were really meant to believe that people mentioned in the Bible were physically attractive. And then they wonder whether they're sinning when they conjure such pictures to go along with Bible verses. But they worry in vain. The Bible will never cause us to sin. We shouldn't feel uncomfortable thinking about physically attractive biblical heroes and heroines if they are described that way in the Bible.

God gave us the ability to be attracted to the physical characteristics of another person. It was all part of His plan for us. Bodies are okay. They are not sin objects. They are not lust objects. No body God has made is a cause for sin.

So if it's fine, and sometimes even necessary, to think about physical attractiveness, am I suggesting Christians have permission to lust? Can we drive out to the beach and become voyeurs for Jesus? Can we rush down to the corner store and buy the latest copy of *Playboy*? After all, we're only following the physical attractions God has given us. The answer is absolutely not.

THERE IS NO WORD FOR LOVE IN THE NEW TESTAMENT THAT HAS ANYTHING WHATSOEVER TO DO WITH LUST, NOT EVEN A HINT OR A SUGGESTION OF IT.

I have read Christian books, though, that suggest that lust is one form of love God made. Maybe you've read them, too. These books say things like: There is "agape" love, unconditional and sacrificial. It is a pure love. Next there is "philo" love. This kind of love is friendship or soulish love. Then there is "eros." We get the word *erotic* from eros. *Erotic* means sexual love, or a feeling of lust for another person. It is powerful. But such reasoning with regards to lust is wrong to the core. There is no word for love in the New Testament that has anything whatsoever to do with lust, not even a hint or a suggestion of it.

Because so many of us don't recognize that God gave us a gift of attraction, we don't have any idea how it works. And since we don't know how it works, we are easily confused and look to the world to define for us what is "normal."

I remember when I was having a problem with lust and the Holy Spirit began to convict me on it. I wanted to be freed from it, so I went to my youth pastor and told him about my problem. This was not an easy thing for me to do. It took weeks to work up the courage. When I finally blurted out my problem and asked him to pray with me, he put his hand on my shoulder and said, "You know, Dean, this just shows that all your parts are in good working order. We are all a bit like that."

I was shocked. I wanted to protest to the youth pastor and say, "I don't want to feel like that. It makes me feel dirty inside." But how could I? If I was to believe my youth pastor, this was a normal condition for a Christian to find himself in. The world tells us lust is okay, and the church often nods its head and says, "Well, yes, we're all a bit like that." But sexual immorality, impurity, and debauchery all involve lust, and those who practice such things will not inherit the kingdom of God:

> The acts of the sinful nature are obvious: sexual immorality, impurity and debauchery; idolatry and witchcraft; hatred, discord, jealousy, fits of rage, selfish ambition, dissensions, factions and envy; drunkenness, orgies, and the like. I warn you, as I did before, that those who live like this will not inherit the kingdom of God. (Galatians 5:19–21)

We need to wake up. We do not take our directions from the world; we take them from the Word of God. Physical attraction is not the same as lust. Lust is not normal. Unfortunately, too many Christians have concluded that because just about everyone lusts it must be normal.

I visited another pastor sometime later when miniskirts were all the rage. I confessed to him that I was having trouble looking at women in miniskirts without lusting. He gave me another piece of misguided advice: "Don't look." He even trotted out a Bible verse—"I have made a covenant with mine eyes that I will not look upon a maid"—to back himself up.

It sounded scriptural, and I thought, well, that's it. I cannot look at women anymore because if I look at a woman, I have lusted. I held my head up high and tried not to look at women. Trouble was, I kept bumping into the walls!

Then I began to wonder, if God created the female body, why couldn't I look at it? Looking and lusting cannot be the same thing. It must be possible to look at something a pure and holy God created without lusting.

So why do we get so confused about lust and attraction? Why do we have such a hard time distinguishing between the two? Defining exactly what the two terms mean helps clears up the confusion.

What exactly is lust? Lust is degrading another person to the sum of their body parts. It is seeing them as less than the unique and complete person God created them to be. Lust is a sin, an aberration. Righteousness, not lust, is the norm for a Christian. We do not have to be "a bit like that" when it comes to lust.

ATTRACTION IS THE ACKNOWLEDGMENT THAT SOMETHING IS PLEASANT.

Attraction is the acknowledgment that something is pleasant. We say things like, "I can't wait for dinner, it smells so good," or "Come outside and look at the sunset, it's spectacular." We say, "He's a great-looking guy," or "She's stunning." These are statements of fact. They're not wrong or sinful. In them we are merely articulating that something is attractive to us.

Now lust involves attraction, but it goes further than that. Lust is attraction plus the desire for selfish gratification at the expense of another human being. We must understand this distinction.

How does this distinction between lust and attraction work out in real-life situations? Imagine a pretty woman walking down the street while a man is walking along the street in the other direction. As he approaches the woman, the man thinks to himself, "Hey, that is a pretty woman." He has not committed a sin in thinking this; he is functioning normally. But if he starts thinking, "I wonder what she looks like without her clothes on. I wonder what it would be like to get in bed with her," then he has crossed the line from attraction to lust. Now he has begun to use the woman to feed his own desires. He is no longer loving this neighbor, but using her selfishly.

Remember in chapter two we talked about the value of the baby on the floor? The woman walking down the street has value. Value, we pointed out, is a function of origin and purpose. Every person on this earth is created by God with the purpose of loving and worshiping Him. Lust devalues human beings.

Have you wondered why women say, "I feel like an object. He looks at me like I'm in a cattle auction?" Women often feel like this because in the eyes of a luster, they *are* an object. They are just a collection of body parts that a man wants to use to satiate his own desires.

EACH PERSON IS VALUABLE BECAUSE HE IS MADE IN THE IMAGE OF GOD FOR FELLOWSHIP WITH GOD, EVEN IF HE IS NOT WALKING IN THAT FELLOWSHIP.

This all comes back to the Christian view of human beings. In the Christian worldview, each person is valuable because he or she is made in the image of God for fellowship with God, even if he or she is not walking in that fellowship. Take the topic of sexual harassment. People object to sexual harassment because they say it is dehumanizing. What do they mean by this? They mean that another person has ceased to see them as a complete human being with personality, emotions, and free will. Instead, that person sees them as an object to be consumed. But if sex is nothing more than my chemicals reacting with your chemicals, how can it be dehumanizing? Doesn't our sexuality work the same way as a cow's? Do cows think they're being sexually harassed by bulls? I don't think so. So why, as human beings, do we think we need to be treated with dignity and decency when it comes to sexual issues? It is because we have value. The whole concept of sexual harassment is based upon the value of human beings, and that value is derived because God created us for a purpose.

OVERINFLATED PHYSICAL ATTRACTION

In our culture we have elevated the value of physical attractiveness beyond what its value actually is. Does this mean that physical attractiveness is of no value? Of course not. Think of it like this. I have a dollar bill in my wallet. Now this dollar bill has value, but if we listen to our parents we will know that the dollar was once worth a lot more than it is now. The perceived value of the dollar in my wallet has been falsely inflated because that dollar will no longer purchase the same goods it did twenty-five years ago. We have inflated physical attractiveness in the same way. Physical attractiveness has value, but today society tells us that value is much higher. It has been artificially inflated to appear more valuable than it really is.

I remember when I first visited Hawaii. I was speaking at a Christian community, and I was invited to stay for lunch. I sat next to a stunningly beautiful woman. We started talking, and she told me she was a former Miss Hawaii who had ranked very high in the Miss America contest. I didn't find this hard to believe. The woman told me she had just recently become a Christian, and then she went on. "All my life I have been beautiful, and men have fallen over themselves to try to date me. I've always had as many boyfriends as I wanted. If I told a guy I liked him, he would drop his current girlfriend just to take me out.

Married men were hitting on me all the time, saying they would leave their wife if I'd date them. I've been showered with so many expensive gifts I've lost count of them. All my girlfriends were jealous of me, and I've been with every type of man I ever wanted to be with. I was even married once." Her voice trailed off at this point, and she started to cry. A minute or two later she continued. "Now I'm a new Christian, and I do not have a boyfriend or a husband, but for the first time in my life I am enjoying meaningful and satisfying relationships with men. No one could ever get past the way I looked, even when I was married to them or sleeping with them. I always knew they were infatuated with my looks and didn't care about what was inside."

That's exactly how the world has overinflated the value of being attractive on the outside over the value of inner attraction. In the world, a person is worth dating, or even marrying, solely because of how he or she looks. How a person looks determines whether he or she is a "good catch." But this is so contrary to the way God wants us to view people. None of us wants other people to relate to us solely because of how we look. Something within us instinctively rises up and says, "Hey, that's shallow. There's a lot more to me than my blonde hair (or biceps)." God gave us our physical form, and He gave others an attraction to it, but He does not intend for physical features to be overemphasized in our relationships.

We cheat ourselves and we cheat the other person if we cannot get beyond the way another person looks. In so doing, the person becomes an object to us instead of a whole person.

It's impossible to fall in love with someone at first sight. When people say it was love at first sight, what they really mean is that they were immediately physically attracted to the other person. Then, because of the physical attraction, they got to know the person better and found that they had grown to love that person as a whole human being in the process. God made us to be attracted to people's insides as well as their outsides.

THE ATTRACTION GIFT OPERATES TOWARDS THE NONPHYSICAL

What does it mean that God has also given us the gift of attraction towards the nonphysical part of a person? Simply put, the nonphysical is whatever is no longer in a person after the person has died. When we look into a coffin, we talk about seeing the person's body, not the person himself or herself. The real person is no longer there. When a person is dead, the intellect, imagination, humor, spirit, personality, and character are gone, and what is left is the body.

If God has planned for us to be attracted to the nonphysical parts of a person, does this mean that the way a person looks on the outside doesn't matter? No. We have already seen that God has given us the ability to be attracted to the outside of a person, but if we stop there and do not also check whether we are attracted to the inside of the person, we will end up shortchanging the person and ourselves. It's like going to one of those parties where everyone brings a gift to swap with someone else. We look at all the gifts and get to choose one without opening it. We choose the one with the gift wrapping that appeals to us and hope we are going to like what's inside. We may or may not be as attracted to what's inside the gift as we are to the outside. In a best-case scenario, the outside of the gift was attractive to us, and when we opened it up, so was what was inside. This is what God wants for us in relationships. While it is part of God's gifting that we are attracted to the physical body, that attraction should never eclipse our attraction for the person living inside.

THE ATTRACTION GIFT HAS BOTH A ROMANTIC AND NONROMANTIC PART

Here, I'm not talking about sexual attraction. It's hard to define romantic attraction. The best definition I have been able to come up with was one supplied by my teenage foster daughter. I heard her on the phone one day talking to one of her girlfriends. She said, "No, I don't like him *like that*." I knew exactly what she was trying to say. She liked him, but not *like that*. Romantic attraction is when we do like someone else *like that*.

In the following chapter we will look more closely at this romantic attraction because it fulfills an important function in our relationships. But to finish this chapter, let me summarize. In designing us to be attracted to other people, God has given us a tremendous gift. When this attraction gift is used appropriately, we can be sure attraction will not lead us to sin. Rather it can lead us into deep, fulfilling, and rewarding relationships with other people.

✎ Chapter Six

THE ROMANTIC GIFT

We have seen in the previous chapter that God has put within us an attraction gift. We ended the chapter by observing that a part of this attraction gift is the ability to become linked to another person romantically. I call this the romantic gift, and it has several aspects we need to explore.

The first thing to notice about romantic attraction is that it is singular in focus. Have you ever noticed you're not romantically attracted to five people at a time? Sometimes you might be attracted to a couple of people for a very short time, but the tussle in your heart doesn't last long, and one person emerges as the one you are interested in. It is not possible for a person to be romantically linked with five people at the same time, unless over time the person has perverted the gift of attraction so much that it becomes distorted. Now, don't get me wrong. I'm not saying we will be romantically attracted to only one person in our entire life. I'm just saying that it will be one person at a time.

The singular nature of the gift of romantic attraction is borne out in the Bible. Remember in Genesis how Jacob worked seven years for his father-in-law so he could marry Rachel? Laban tricked him and gave him Leah to be his wife instead. What did Jacob do? He turned right around and promised to work another seven years for Rachel because Rachel was the one for whom he had the romantic attraction.

A second thing to remember about romantic attraction is that we are in control of it. This is an important point. God has designed us with the ability to control our romantic attractions. These attractions are not beyond our control. They can and must be directed by our will in accordance with the Word of God. Romantic attraction can and must be directed by our choice.

Let me put this is real terms. You don't *have* to be in love with anybody. Of course, the world tells us differently. You've heard the songs that convey messages like, "You made me love you even though I didn't want to," and, "I was walking down the street and bam, it hit me."

This notion that love is something that hits us is a lie. Romantic love is not induced by a chubby little angel flying around shooting people with love arrows without their knowing it until it's too late for them to resist. Let me repeat, we don't have to be in love with anybody. Our romantic gift can and must be directed by our will.

FALLING IN LOVE WITH THE WRONG PERSON DOES NOT HAVE TO HAPPEN.

Notice I didn't say it can be initiated by our will, only that it can be directed. We can't walk up to someone and make ourselves feel romantically attracted to the person. Our romantic attraction gift finds candidates for us, people with whom we could "fall in love." The next step is a deliberate choice. Either we choose to pursue the person our attraction gift has singled out as a candidate or we choose not to pursue the person. We are never forced to have to pursue anyone.

Of course, we can fool ourselves into thinking we are not pursuing someone while all the while we have rearranged our life to be near the person, or we kid ourselves into really believing that we're meeting with the person over lunch to discuss a class assignment. But if we are honest in our heart, we know that one, we are attracted to the person, and two, we are acting on that attraction.

It is also possible to be in love with the wrong person. It happens all the time. Can a person be in love with someone of the same sex? Yes. Can a Christian be in love with an unsaved person? Yes. Can a person be in love with someone who is already married? Yes. All of these things are possible, but that doesn't mean they have to happen. Such things happen only if we allow them to happen. It is not "fate," and it is not inevitable. Falling in love with the wrong person does not have to happen. We are not the victims of attraction, but participants in it.

Two criteria are essential before Christians act on an attraction. First, Christians must apply God's truth to the situation. The Bible says I am not to be romantically linked to someone of the same sex. I can be nonromantically linked to the person, but not romantically. The Bible also says not to commit adultery. So I am forbidden to be romantically linked to a person who is married to someone else. Second, when our romantic ability finds us a candidate, we must seek the Lord. We need to ask whether this is the right time and the right person He wants us to pursue.

You might say, "You can't just choose this stuff. If it happens it happens." No. If I were to ask you if you'd ever murder someone, you would tell me no, of course not. You would never murder anyone. You would rather kill yourself than kill someone else. But how can I be sure? What if a situation occurred that made you really mad and you wanted to kill the person involved? Would you take an ax and hack the person to pieces? Or what if a woman left her purse next to you on a bus; would you steal it? How can you be sure you wouldn't? You can be sure you wouldn't murder or steal because such things are repulsive to you. You know you're not that sort of person. So you are not walking in pride when you say you wouldn't murder. Instead, you are walking in the accurate knowledge of God's laws and your own conscience. You have closed the door to stealing or murder. In the same way, you need to close the door to being in love with the wrong person. You do not have to become involved in homosexual relationships or commit adultery.

When are people most likely to become involved in a relationship with the wrong person? When they say to themselves, "I wouldn't mind doing that if the right opportunity came along." Guess what? Satan is right there waiting with just the right opportunity to present to us. If we're open to it, I guarantee it will happen. But if we refuse to accept it as a option, it does not have to happen, and it will not happen. We do not have to live in fear that such a thing will happen to us.

The flip side of this is that we do not have to fall out of love with a person. Falling out of love is a choice, too. We've all heard stories like this: "I rolled over in bed one morning and looked at George, and I realized it was gone! There wasn't anything left. You have to be honest with yourself, when it's over, it's over. You can't bring back the magic. You can't stay together just for the sake of the kids."

You have to be honest with yourself are the dumbest words ever uttered. They are the excuse for more heartache than any other words. We ought to be honest not to ourselves but to something much greater. We must be honest to the truth.

When a person says, "I woke up and it was gone," what does she mean? George is obviously still there, even if he is snoring. The bed is still there. So what is the "it" she's talking about? How does "it" leave, and where does "it" go?

Today, many young married couples trying to figure out relationships get scared by the idea of love's being an "it." They think, "Let me get this straight. There's an 'it,' and this 'it' can leave anytime. I have no control over 'it,' and when 'it' is gone the only honest thing to do is admit the marriage is over, rip the children away from their father (or mother), and go off and find myself. What if 'it' leaves during the wedding or the honeymoon? What about a year later?" No wonder people today don't bother to get married. Marriage is way too risky if you believe love is an "it" that can vanish at any moment.

If God had designed us this way, we could take Him to court as a rip-off artist. Why? Because He would be telling us marriage is for life and that we are to honor and submit to each other in love while at the same time making it impossible for us to control who we love.

There are times in most romantic relationships when we will have to remind ourselves to stay in love with the person we have chosen. Imagine, for example, you are a man getting ready for work in the morning and your wife is in the kitchen fixing breakfast. You hear her yell, "Get out here, you're late again. You're always late for breakfast." So you hurry out into the kitchen, and she says, "Why are you wearing that suit? It makes you look fat. Oh, and you never took out the garbage." The morning continues, and you finally escape the house and enter the organized world of your office. Your secretary greets you at the door with a cup of coffee. She asks you how your weekend went and laughs at your new joke. She tells you what she thinks of the latest football game, and you find her views so interesting you ask her out to lunch to discuss them in more depth.

And where does all this lead? Two months later you are telling your wife, "Honey, it's over. I didn't want it to happen, but I'm in love with my secretary. We're going to move in together and get married." Do you think this scenario is far-fetched? Or that it doesn't happen to Christians?

My family attended a church for a long time and in the process got very close to another family at the church. The wife was the pianist, and her husband was the head usher. Both of them had been in the church all their lives, growing up through the Sunday school and youth group. They had married and had two beautiful girls. One day I got a phone call at my office. It was the husband telling me he had to see me over lunch. We made arrangements and met at a particular restaurant. Over our soup and salad, my friend told me, "I'm leaving my wife."

"What's wrong?" I asked, shocked. "Are you crazy? You have everything going for you."

"I know," he said, "but you don't understand. I'm in love with another woman."

I looked him right in the eye. "Don't be in love with another woman."

"Dean, you don't get it," he insisted. "I'm in love with another woman."

I repeated myself, but it was no use. Even though my friend had sat in the front row of church all of his life, he had allowed his mind to be molded by the belief that you can fall in love and out of love with anyone at any time and that there is absolutely nothing you can do about it. He thought it was totally out of his control.

I tried another approach in the hope I could talk some sense into the man. "What are you going to tell your two little girls?"

He shrugged his shoulders. "I don't know. I hope they will understand as they get older."

I wanted to yell, understand what? That their father had so little commitment to their mother that he allowed himself to indulge his feelings and his passion and put himself in a position where he fell in love with another woman?

Over the years I've noticed an interesting thing in my own marriage and the marriages of many people I counsel. Feelings come and feelings go. That's a fact. Sometimes we can feel head over heels about our spouse, and other times everything seems dull. But if we stay committed through the dull times, the feelings of love return. But if, like my friend, we choose to withdraw our commitment from our spouse and give it to someone else, the relationship is doomed. Sometimes this withdrawal of commitment may be so subtle no one else notices, but we know where our heart is and whether we are letting it run after another person.

A marriage is a lot like being a Christian. Suppose tomorrow morning I wake up and feel unsaved. I don't feel one bit of love for God. I try to read the Bible, but it's boring. I try to concentrate in church, but my mind keeps wandering to what I had for dinner. Have you ever had days like that? I have. Now, if I walk on and keep committed to the Lord even though I lack a lot of feelings, eventually the feelings return. I go back to knowing I am saved, and I enjoy reading my Bible again. If, however, I act on my feelings and stop going to church, reading my Bible, and praying, it is most likely that the feelings will not return and I will give up Christianity. It happens all the time.

The same is true regarding falling in and out of love. It is not something outside of our control, something that comes over us and takes our will away. Paul makes it clear that nothing has this level of control over a Christian.

> Two or three prophets should speak, and the others should weigh carefully what is said. And if a revelation comes to someone who is sitting down, the first speaker should stop. For you can all prophesy in turn so that everyone may be instructed and encouraged. The spirits of prophets are subject to the control of prophets. For God is not a God of disorder but of peace." (1 Corinthians 14:29–33)

The spirits of prophets are subject to the control of prophets, and to this we could add, the spirits of lovers are subject to the control of lovers.

If we are to become mature Christians, we must bring our will under the direction of the God of peace and order. I am not saying that people are not "in love" with people of their same sex. I am saying that because of the way God has made us, it doesn't need to happen. What about married people? Does a married man have to fall in love with another woman? No. If it happens, it is because he lets it happen. Does a married woman have to fall in love with another man? Not at all. It happens if she indulges her fantasies and allows her affections to run wild until falling in love with another man seems inevitable—but it is not. We do not live in a fatalistic world where things "just happen." We live in a world designed by a careful, loving Creator. That Creator made humans to rule according to truth, not to be ruled.

Remember, romantic attraction is both singular and controllable. Romantic affection does not control us and lead us around by the nose. We do not have to fall in love or out of love. We can choose to control the gift God has given us.

Chapter Seven

LOGICAL AND LOVING LIMITS

As humans we exercise power in so many ways. We have physical power that we can exert over others. God gave each of us hands, and we can choose to use those hands to give a gift or to punch someone in the face, to comfort a child or to steal a man's wallet.

We have a powerful intellect, which we can use to invent a new machine to help people who are sick or disabled or to plan the most diabolical crime of the century. It's the same intellect, just channeled in different directions.

Our personality is also powerful. We can use it to manipulate others, or we can use it to influence others to righteousness.

We have sexual power, too. While many Christians might understand the other forms of power available to them as human beings, they don't understand their sexuality. Indeed, many wish their hormones would dry up when they become Christians. But they don't. They're just as powerful as they were before. Some Christians rationalize that because God gave us hormones and feelings He must mean for us to have sex outside the boundaries of marriage. But that is like saying God gave me a hand, so He must mean for me to punch you, or God gave me an intellect, so He must mean for me to use it to rip you off in a business deal.

GOD GIVES US GOOD GIFTS, AND HE CHARGES US WITH CHANNELING THEM INTO PURPOSEFUL AND LOVING ACTS.

You've probably at one time or another overheard a Christian in a nasty argument. Afterwards the person tries to explain himself. He says something like, "God wouldn't have given me a mouth if He didn't expect me to use it." At first this might sound okay. God did make the person's mouth and gave the person the ability to speak. Even so, we feel violated to hear a Christian (or anyone else, for that matter) speak this way to another person. Why? Because we recognize that the person with the gift should be in control of the gift, and not vice versa. There is no excuse for Christians to slander or abuse another person, and for them to blame their actions on God is a cop-out. God gives us good gifts, and He charges us with channeling them into purposeful and loving acts.

Sexual activity is also a powerful gift. We can use it to enhance and strengthen the linkage in marriage, or we can use it to link us to the wrong people and thereby damage marriages and hurt others. As with all gifts He has given us, God expects us to channel sexual activity in the most loving way, both for ourselves and for all others concerned.

When I was a teenager, the standard Christian teaching was "wait until marriage to have sex." Typically, that was as far as the discussion would go. Sex outside of marriage was wrong, and we shouldn't have it, and for the girls, if they had it, there would be lingering physical evidence that they had "gone too far." I still believe that the message to "wait until marriage to have sex" is right, but I wish that Christian leaders back then had explained to us why sex outside of marriage was wrong and how it could affect us.

We serve a God who has reasons for everything He requires of us. He is not some kind of arbitrary being with a warped sense of humor who got up one morning and said, "Ha! Look at those puny human beings. I'm going to give them a powerful sex drive and then forbid them to use it. That should be fun to watch!"

No, God is loving, and He is supremely logical. If He tells us not to do something, He has excellent reasons. Now that doesn't mean that if we don't understand the reasons for something we don't have to do what God asks. We tell small children not to poke metal knives into electric outlets. If they disobey us, they run the risk of being injured by electricity whether or not they understood the reason for our telling them not to do it. Of course, the best prevention is for children to develop intellectually to where they can understand about volts and current and electrons. In this way, children know not only not to put a knife in an outlet but also why they shouldn't. Electricity is powerful, and if it is not used in the right way, it is destructive.

GOD'S LAWS EXIST FOR OUR

ULTIMATE PROTECTION.

In a similar way, sexual activity is very powerful, and if we do not obey God's laws for using it, we can be harmed. And just like the child and the electrical outlet, the bottom line is that God's laws exist for our ultimate protection. Of course, the highest good would be for us to grow in our emotions, intellect, and spirit so that we could understand the underlying principles as well.

This is where we so often go wrong when we try to witness to people. Maybe our friend from college or work is sexually active, and we try to tell her that God says that what she is doing is sin. Her comeback is usually something like, "Well, it's not harming anyone, is it? I mean we're both consenting adults." Or a friend might say, "Christianity might work for you, but I'm a red-blooded male. I have to do what I have to do." Or, "We're committed to each other, a lot more committed than many married couples I know, even Christian ones."

How do we respond to these comebacks? "God made us, and He says sex outside of marriage is wrong, so it must be"? We can say that, and it's true, just as true as saying electricity can kill you. But if we look into the Bible, we find out why and how it is wrong, and knowing this allows us to respond much more intelligently to our friend's challenge.

In 1 Corinthians, Paul gives us some insight into why and how sexual immorality is wrong.

> "Everything is permissible for me"—but not everything is beneficial. "Everything is permissible for me"—but I will not be mastered by anything. "Food for the stomach and the stomach for food"—but God will destroy them both. The body is not meant for sexual immorality, but for the Lord, and the Lord for the body. By his power God raised the Lord from the dead, and he will raise us also. Do you not know that your bodies are members of Christ himself? Shall I then take the members of Christ and unite them with a prostitute? Never! Do you not know that he who unites himself with a prostitute is one with her in body? For it is said, "The two will become one flesh." But he who unites himself with the Lord is one with him in spirit. Flee from sexual immorality. All other sins a man commits are outside his body; but he who sins sexually sins against his own body. Do you not know that your body is a temple of the Holy Spirit, who is in you, whom you have received from God? You are not your own; you were bought at a price. Therefore honor God with your body. (1 Corinthians 6:12–20)

At first glance you might wonder what Paul is talking about here. It seems so mixed up. He tells us he is allowed to do everything but that his body belongs to Jesus and it's going to be destroyed along with the food he has eaten. It all sounds disconnected and unrelated, but in fact it's very logical and helps to answer the "why" question.

To understand what Paul is saying here, we have to understand the people he was writing to. They were the new converts at Corinth, located in Greece. Corinth was a cesspool of sin. You have never heard of anything evil or perverted that did not go on in Corinth. People sometimes say to me, "It was all right to tell Christians to live a sexually pure life in Bible times. It was easy then. What was there to tempt them?" Believe me, there was plenty to tempt people in Corinth, where they even used sexual practices to worship their gods.

Paul visited Corinth and preached the gospel to the unsaved people there. As a result, many Corinthians became Christians. When Paul moved on to preach the gospel in other places, he left some of his helpers behind to help the Corinthians. But he began to hear disturbing things about what the new church at Corinth was allowing. The church had broken into factions in response to the sexual immorality that was all around it.

At one extreme, new converts were saying, "This sexual stuff is dangerous and ungodly. I remember Paul told us our bodies are now holy temples, and I'm not doing anything sexual ever again with my holy temple. It can get out of control too easily, and then I'd be back where I started." As a result of this thinking, husbands and wives separated, and they forbade their adult children to marry.

At the other extreme, a philosophy now known as Greek dualism emerged. Here the Corinthian Christians said to each other, "Hey, this is great. We can do what we want with our bodies. God doesn't care. After all, our bodies are going to rot in the ground. It's our spirits that God is interested in. We can get drunk on communion wine, and we can have sex with whomever we want because it doesn't matter. It's only our body that's affected."

This kind of thinking is still around today. In the 1970s a friend of mine went to a Jesus festival. He saw one young woman there who was worshiping the Lord with all her heart, or so it seemed. She was always at the front of the meetings with her hands raised and her eyes shut. But after the meetings were over, she would light up a joint and crawl into a tent to sleep with her boyfriend. My friend cornered her one day and asked how she could worship Jesus and then do the things she was doing. "You don't understand," she said cheerfully. "Jesus is living in my spirit, but my body will not be saved until the resurrection, so it doesn't really matter what I do with my body."

That's Greek dualism updated!

In the above passage, Paul shows that as long as our bodies are alive, our spirit permeates our physical body making it a temple and making our body parts members of Christ. He says:

> The body is not meant for sexual immorality, but for the Lord, and the Lord for the body. By his power God raised the Lord from the dead, and he will raise us also. Do you not know that your bodies are members of Christ himself? Shall I then take the members of Christ and unite them with a prostitute? Never!

What Paul is saying here is that we cannot function within our body without touching our spirit. We say things like "I asked Jesus into my heart." Do we mean this literally? If I had a heart transplant, would I have to ask Jesus into my new heart? Or does it mean that a non-Christian who received the heart of a dead Christian is born again? Of course not. The heart is a metaphor for our being, intellect, will, and emotions. To get to the heart of a matter means to get to its essence, its center. When we invite Jesus into our hearts, we invite Him to permeate every part of us, to be in us and on us and all around us.

BECAUSE OUR BODIES HOUSE THE HOLY SPIRIT, THE SEXUAL ACT CAN NEVER BE JUST A PHYSICAL THING.

This means I cannot touch a Christian's body without touching the Spirit of Christ, and if I am a Christian, no one can touch my body without touching the Spirit of Christ. We are living temples of the most high God. And because our bodies house the Holy Spirit, the sexual act can never be just a physical thing.

Today we often hear people categorize sexual activity. "Oh, well, that was just a one-night stand" or "There is sex with love and commitment, and then there are sexual encounters, you know, casual sex."

This concept of casual sex has become popular. It refers to a kind of sex people have before they have serious sex. It comes with no strings attached and is sort of like exercising. You have the body parts, why not keep them in working order? Or, as one woman laughed and said when a friend told her both she and her fiancé were virgins, "Hey, I wouldn't want to buy a new car without taking it for a test drive!" So casual sex is like test driving a car before you commit to buy it?

SEX IS NEVER JUST A PHYSICAL ACT. IT IS THE MESHING OF THE MIND, SOUL, EMOTIONS, AND SPIRITS OF TWO PEOPLE.

There is just one big fallacy in this kind of thinking. Paul draws our attention to it in the context of the above Bible passage. Because our bodies are integrated with our spirit as long as we are alive, when we have sex with somebody it is a total merging of entire being: body, soul, and spirit. When two people are involved sexually, their personalities are totally integrated until the two literally become one.

Try mixing sand and sugar together in a bowl and then separating them again. It is almost impossible to do without leaving some residue of sand and sugar mixed together. This is how sex works, and it is how God designed it to work. In marriage, leaving that residue is beneficial, because it strengthens the oneness that God has supernaturally established.

Sexual activity outside the marriage relationship has devastating effects on both our lives and the lives of those with whom we have sex, because it links us to a person to whom we have not been supernaturally joined. The superficial joining by sex alone is ripped apart after each act, damaging the two participants. That is why sex outside of marriage is neither loyal nor loving. In the next chapter, we will look specifically at what damage sexual immorality can cause.

Chapter Eight

DAMAGE DONE

Flee from sexual immorality. All other sins
a man commits are outside his body; but he who
sins sexually sins against his own body.
                    —1 Corinthians 6:18

Once a man sexually interacts with a woman, the two have been designed by God to stay with each other. If they do not, and instead go their own ways, both will be damaged, wounded, and hurt at a very deep level. Neither person will be exactly intact the way he or she was before the sexual encounter took place. I'm not talking about the physical act here. We cannot damage our bodies through normal sexual relations. Sex itself is a normal bodily function. But it can and will damage our emotions, intellect, will, and spirit. Let's look more closely at how this happens.

EVERY ACT OF SEX OUTSIDE OF MARRIAGE DAMAGES BOTH PARTIES INVOLVED

Think of a piece of paper. No matter how carefully you try to rip it, the ripping leaves a jagged edge. The same is true of sexual relations outside of marriage. No matter how smoothly or sensibly you try to extricate yourself from a sexual relationship, even a one-hour encounter with a prostitute, the result is a jagged rip right through the center of who you are.

God has known this all along. He continually reminds us, "Don't do it. You have no idea how much damage you'll do to yourself and to the other person." But we argue back, "God doesn't know how much we love each other, and we're going to get married soon anyway."

SEX OUTSIDE OF MARRIAGE IS WRONG BECAUSE IT BRINGS DAMAGE TO THE PARTICIPANTS.

Sex outside of marriage is wrong because it brings damage to the participants. How would it sound if our boyfriend or girlfriend said to us, "I have to be with you. I need you, I love you. I want to damage you!" It doesn't sound very romantic, does it?

What is it, then, that is damaged when we engage in sex outside of marriage?

Our Mind Is Damaged

When I say our mind is damaged, I don't mean we can no longer get good grades at school. Rather, I mean that after such a sexual encounter, our memories and sensations are in limbo, disjointed and disconnected from relationship with another human being. The person we shared the sex act with no longer wants to be with us or share our dreams for the future. We have the memories but not the reality in our life.

Now we know what it's like to have sex, but we are not committed to a relationship. God did not want us to have those feelings and sensations. It is torture to become aware of something we have to put aside. Sex is a pleasurable experience. Sex outside of marriage used to be called carnal knowledge, and that's a good description of it. After sex we are left with the knowledge of how it feels, and we must carry that knowledge with us. But in doing so, we are carrying something God never intended for us to carry outside the union of marriage.

God's highest plan for us was that every sexual act would be associated with a real human being with whom we were in a committed and lasting relationship. We should have no other sexual experience or knowledge except in relation to that person.

When we have sex outside of marriage, we develop a knowledge of "it." We learn how to do "it." We do "it." But when we do "it," we cheat ourselves. We have taken that which was meant to be intensely personal, and made it general and technical. We are then running around with memories and knowledge that have no context in our lives. The memories are still stimulating and exciting, but the person we shared them with is long gone.

Our Soul Is Damaged

Sex outside of marriage leaves our emotions traumatized, much as they are traumatized after being in a car wreck or experiencing the death of a loved one. After we have had sex outside of marriage, we find our emotions are more exposed. We notice that we get upset more often or cry a lot. We also get angrier at other people and situations than we used to. We have been emotionally ripped apart from the other person. Proverbs asks the question:

> Can a man scoop fire into his lap without his clothes being burned? Can a man walk on hot coals without his feet being scorched? (Proverbs 6:27–28)

This is not just a figure of speech. I have talked to numerous people who have told me that after they had sex outside of marriage they felt wounded inside. They told me they felt as if someone had punched them in the stomach and winded them. I say to them, "You damaged yourself. You sinned against your being."

If we engage in enough illicit sex, our emotions will become so damaged we no longer have the capacity to love others or to be sensitive to their needs. Have you ever met someone who is very promiscuous or sexually active? Were you struck with how sensitive the person was? How well-adjusted? Did the person have a deep personality and an inspirational character? I don't think so. Every single sexual act outside of marriage damages the person involved in it. The cumulative effect of these acts can create hardened, shallow, angry, insecure people.

Our Will Is Damaged

Not only are our emotions damaged, but our will is damaged, too. The human will is very strong—it's like a steel reinforcing rod. It seems like it would be impossible to break a reinforcing rod with our bare hands, but there is a way it can be done, and quite easily. All we have to do is bend the rod back and forth in one spot. At first it takes a lot of energy to bend it even a little, but eventually the rod begins to soften up. If we keep at it, eventually the reinforcing rod will break in two.

The strongest part of the human will is in the area of sexuality. We have been designed with a great deal of determination in this area. But over time, if we let it happen, our will, just like the steel reinforcing rod, can be defeated. With each successive breaking of our will in relation to sex outside of marriage, it becomes easier and easier to break it the next time.

Some men have difficulty in dealing with the will. They don't seem to get it. Maybe the man has been dating and sleeping with a woman for a while and then she decides she doesn't want to go out with him anymore. A week later he breaks into her apartment and rapes her. "What's the big deal?" he questions. After all, he'd had sex with the same woman in the same bed a week ago, and she loved it. So why does she file a rape complaint with the police this time?

It is because rape is an act of sex that is carried out against the will of the other person. The person did not agree to it and so feels violated and used. Sometimes previously sexually active people who have been raped take a lifetime to get over being raped because their will was violated. Something was taken from them that they can never get back.

Now if someone kidnapped you and forced you to eat something you hated, such as broccoli, or made you swim in the sea when you don't like salt water, you would certainly feel violated, but nothing like the feeling of violation a rape victim experiences. The trauma of rape shows us just how strongly the will guards our sexual experiences and how hard the experience is to overcome when a person is forced into having sex against her will.

SEX OUTSIDE OF MARRIAGE IS UNCOMMITTED SEX

I was teaching in a Discipleship Training School one time when a woman got to her feet as I spoke about the damage sex outside of marriage can do. I could see she was very angry at what I'd said, so I let her speak. She began, "I cannot allow you to continue to heap condemnation on all of us and force us to agree with your opinions. I had sex with a lot with guys before I became a Christian, and it never hurt me any! What difference does a little piece of paper make if we were committed to each other? What's marriage got to do with it?"

IF YOU ARE NOT MARRIED YOU ARE NOT COMMITTED, BECAUSE MARRIAGE IS THE COMMITMENT.

By the time she was finished she was almost yelling. Her belligerent attitude changed the whole atmosphere of the room. I could see the rest of the students sitting on the edge of their seats, wondering, "Yeah, what is wrong with sex within a committed relationship?"

For a moment I didn't know how to answer the woman, and then something came to me that I had never consciously processed. "My dear," I said. "If you are not married you are not committed, because marriage is the commitment."

I began to think about what I had said. It must have been inspiration because it made total sense! It doesn't matter where you live, if you jump over a stick in the jungle somewhere or you wear a white dress down the aisle, you are married. But regardless of what culture you are a part of, marriage can be summed up in one word: *commitment*.

So, to the next person who suggests you have sex with him, say you want to have sex only with a person who is one hundred percent committed to you and to whom you are committed one hundred percent. Watch the person's eyes light up. "Oh, yes, baby, I'm one hundred percent committed to you. Let's do it."

Next say to the person, "That's great. When do you want to get married?" Now watch the person's face drop and listen as the person says something like "Well I'd like to, baby, but I have to get through college first," or "I don't think I'm ready for that type of heavy duty commitment," or "I don't want to settle down yet. I want to travel and see the world some."

Where is the one hundred percent commitment now? It evaporated in the face of reality. It never was one hundred percent commitment. If it had been, the person would have been glad to seal the commitment with marriage vows.

It is naive to assume a person is committed if he or she is not prepared to back it up. Say, for example, I wanted to build you a house. I say to you, "Give me one hundred thousand dollars because I want to build you a house." You would say to me, "You're crazy. Give me some details. How big is the house going to be? Where are the plans for it? Do you have a lot to build it on?"

"Trust me," I say. "I'm committed to building you this house. I feel I am going to build it. I'm really committed to seeing it through. I will do whatever it takes to build this house for you."

So you say to me, "Okay, I'll have my lawyer draw up a contract. You can sign it in front of a witness, and then I'll give you half the money."

I say, "Now that's so cold and clinical. Don't you believe me when I tell you I want to build you a house? Don't you trust me? I am totally committed. Come on, give me the money. I want to get started."

You would be crazy to give me a penny. Why? Because if I really was committed to building you a house, I would have no trouble signing a contract to seal the deal. The witnessed contract would be the proof of my commitment. Nothing less would do.

The same is true for a sexual relationship. It needs to take place after a public commitment in front of witnesses has occurred. That commitment is marriage.

Traditionally, the Maori people of New Zealand had a different way of getting married. In the days before Europeans arrived in the country, a young man would raise his eyebrows at a young woman. If she liked him, they would stroll off into the bush together. There they would have sex. But when they got back to the village, the tribal elders would have prepared a wedding ceremony for them. The man and the woman had to get married right then, and if the man left the woman, her family would hunt him down and kill him. (Now that's commitment at work!)

ANY SEX OUTSIDE OF THE COMMITMENT OF MARRIAGE IS UNPROTECTED SEX.

MARRIAGE PROVIDES A CIRCLE OF SPIRITUAL PROTECTION

I am tired of hearing about Christian teenagers who are having sex. I am especially tired of hearing about "responsible" adults who counsel them and ask if they use a condom. When the teenager says yes, the "caring" adult lets out a loud sigh of relief. You can almost hear what he's thinking. "No matter what else they did, at least they didn't have unprotected sex." I want to tell you that's exactly what they had. Any sex outside of the commitment of marriage is unprotected sex.

What are these young people unprotected from? The devil. He has never missed an act of fornication in history. I have been on every inhabited continent, and I can tell you that sex outside of marriage is rampant everywhere I go. Because of its destructiveness, illicit sex is one of the biggest problems facing humanity. Sex in the wrong context destroys thousands of lives every day. The life of a woman who wakes up to find her husband has left her for another woman is crushed. Children who are abandoned by one or the other of their parents are permanently scarred psychologically. Young women who are raped by their dates are devastated by it. The list could go on and on. We only have to watch the nightly news to see the destructive power uncontrolled sex has in people's lives.

In the marriage ceremony, God Himself is in attendance. He witnesses and seals the commitment a man and a woman make to each other. In many ways, getting married mirrors being saved. The two words *I do* change a person forever. That might sound strange; after all, they're just words. But they are words that signify a transaction that takes place in the spiritual realm. When we accepted the Lord Jesus Christ, we believed in our heart, confessed with our mouth, and what happened? A transaction took place in the heavenlies, and we were saved. A similar thing happens at a wedding. The two people involved love each other in their hearts and confess it with their mouths. When they do that, something happens at that moment.

> But in the beginning of creation God made them male and female. For this reason a man will leave his father and mother and be united to his wife, and the two will become one flesh. So they are no longer two, but one. Therefore what God has joined together, let man not separate. (Mark 10:6–9)

Most people think a couple is really joined at the motel on their honeymoon. But these verses contradict this notion. Jesus tells us that it is God, not sex, who joins a couple together.

Hebrews 13:4 tells us that "the marriage bed is undefiled." Undefiled is a strange way to describe marriage. The Greek root word for undefiled indicates the potential for demonic activity. So the statement that the marriage bed is undefiled means that the devil cannot interfere with sexual activities within a marriage because they are under the protection of God. God's hedge of protection around a marriage is called a covenant. Within the covenant a couple is secure and safe, as are any children born to the couple. Any sex outside that covenant is unprotected from the enemy of our souls. God wanted the sexual relationship to be private and unaccessible to the devil.

While the biggest danger in not being protected lies in giving the enemy access, the physical dangers must also be pointed out. Thousands of people die every week from AIDS, a disease primarily propagated by sexual activity. Venereal diseases such as gonorrhea, chlamydia, herpes, genital warts, and syphilis are at an all time high. When some of these viruses get into your body, they never leave for the rest of your life. Those sexually active early in life are at greater risk of cervical cancer. Unwanted pregnancy has increased not decreased in this day of so-called protected sex. Many of the so-called protections are not as effective as we are told, and even with them, disease and death are reaching epidemic proportions. Abiding by God's limits is still the only logical and loving way to stem this tide and to protect ourselves and our neighbors.

SEX IS AN ACT OF INTIMACY

Let's assume you love to take a good shower, the kind where you have two shower heads spraying water on you, and you have scented soap, soft music in the background, and fluffy white towels waiting for you to dry off when you're done. Now think about taking one of those showers in the demonstration model set up in the middle of a busy hardware store. "No way," you say. But why? I thought you loved to take showers. And here you have the chance to shower in the luxury model with gold-plated fixtures. You tell me the reason you wouldn't take a shower there is that taking a shower in the middle of a store destroys the intimacy of the experience. It no longer is a pleasant experience for you.

Let me give you another example. You could choose to have a special date at the central Tokyo train station in Japan. Thousands of people are pushing and shoving, trying to get into trains. Some of the guards have long, broomlike instruments that they use to push people tightly together so they can cram more people into each train car. You have barely enough space to lift your arms.

Or the other hand, you could choose to take your date to a quiet restaurant overlooking a beautiful harbor. A candle flickers on your table, casting around little pools of light. Your table is in a corner of the restaurant away from everyone else.

I think all of us would choose the restaurant for our date. It would be almost impossible to have an intimate date at the Tokyo train station.

What is intimacy then? It is sharing something personal with only one other person.

Sex was designed to be engaged in in intimacy with one other person to whom we are linked in a marriage commitment. Once we have had sex outside of this commitment, things can never be like they were when we shared the act of sex in the context of just one lover. I'm not saying God can't repair the damage done or bring redemption into the situation. Of course He can. But even He cannot undo the act we have done. God intended sex to be something we enjoy with only one person.

PREPARATION AND EXPERIENCE ARE WORLDS APART. ANYONE WHO IS GOING TO GET MARRIED NEEDS TO BE PREPARED FOR SEXUAL INTIMACY.

ILLICIT SEX CAN PUT A WEIGHT ON OUR MARRIAGE

I have read sex manuals written by humanists, and many of them imply that it would be humiliating to arrive at your wedding night and not know what to do. These writers trot out fictitious stories about people like Joe and Susie from New Jersey and how neither of them had any experience before they were married. Their wedding night was a complete disaster, and it took therapy to straighten them out after the horrible experience. The article or book typically ends with a statement that presumes that being prepared and being experienced are the same thing when it comes to sex. But preparation and experience are worlds apart. Anyone who is going to get married needs to be prepared for sexual intimacy. He or she should go to a doctor for a checkup and know what is going to happen. But that's a long way from needing to have prior experience.

I do not specialize in marriage counseling, but I have talked with hundreds of pastors and marriage counselors, and I have taken my own informal survey with them. I ask them whether they find that people say they have had serious difficulty in their marriage because they lacked prior sexual experience. They all just shook their heads. I have never heard of one single person who had trouble sexually through lack of prior experience. If we're married, we've all had a first time for sex. Often this first experience is awkward and strange. Why would anyone want to have that experience with someone who is not in love with or committed to him or her? There are multiplied thousands of girls who have sex for the first time believing they are in an intimate setting with someone who is committed to them, only to find every detail of their night's encounter being laughed at in class the next day. This is devastating. Sex is something we get better at with practice. Because of this, we want to practice it with someone who is committed to us in every way, and that means in marriage.

Premarital sex puts a weight on a marriage. What is that weight? It is guilt. Sexual sin is the hardest thing to get over. It is amazing how many people carry a residue of guilt into their marriages. They carry this guilt burden not because they believe God can't forgive them but because they find it so difficult to forgive themselves.

Others carry fear into their marriages. They believe that bad things will happen to them because God is angry at them for the wrong things they've done. I have sat with people who sincerely believed that their baby's birth defects or their constant miscarriages were the result of sexual sin. But it was simply not true. There is only one payment for sin, and that is death. If you have taken Christ as your savior, you have moved from death to life. There is no more punishment, although there may be consequences. If you get pregnant from an affair and then become a Christian, you will still be pregnant after you accept Christ. But God has no desire to arrange our lives in such a way as to punish us for things we did before we knew Him.

This is all easy to say, but if a person is riddled with remorse for sexual sin, sometimes it is very difficult to accept that the situations in his or her life are not some sort of pay back for what he or she did. Such people need a lot of support to get around this issue, which is a burden no marriage ought to have to bear.

SEX OUTSIDE OF MARRIAGE DESTROYS TRUST

Bill and Lucy are in love and plan to get married. They are both Christians, but Bill argues over and over that God has made him with certain needs and unless those needs are met, he doesn't think he can hold on until their wedding date in the summer. Bill loves Lucy so much, but he has to have "it" now. Lucy is afraid she will lose Bill if she does not give in, and besides she is eager to have sex, too. So secretly they have sex until they get married.

Two years later, Bill's work sends him to Europe for three months. Lucy spends the whole time imagining that Bill is having sex with some European woman or a succession of women. She wonders whether he will be able to control his "needs" when she is not there to meet them.

Ten years later, Lucy is in the hospital. She has had to have a breast removed and is on chemotherapy. Her hair is falling out, and she is depressed. And guess what? On top of all her problems, she is worried that Bill is going to hit on his new secretary at work. Why is she worried this way? Because Bill still has sexual needs, and as he used to tell her with a wink, a man has to do what he has to do.

IF YOU AND YOUR SPOUSE HAVE
A TRACK RECORD OF SELF–CONTROL IN
THE AREA OF SEXUAL RELATIONSHIPS,
YOU WILL HAVE A MORE OPEN AND
TRUSTING RELATIONSHIP.

Any marriage goes through difficulties, but what a burden it is to have to wonder whether your spouse is being faithful to you based on his or her past performance. Any sex previous to marriage can increase suspicion and accusation in the marriage. I've seen marriages split up, not because a partner committed adultery but because a suspicious partner could not believe that his or her spouse did not commit adultery.

Marriage is so much more meaningful and uncomplicated when we can say to our spouse, "You know, I have always been committed to your highest good. I had the self-control not to have sex with you before we were married, and I will always use that same self-control to avoid having sex with anyone else." If you and your spouse have a track record of self-control in the area of sexual relationships, you will have a more open and trusting relationship. That's why self-control is not just discipline, it is love control.

SEX OUTSIDE OF MARRIAGE CREATES COMPARISONS AND UNSUSTAINABLE EXPECTATIONS

A strong young Christian man came to see me one day. He had a beautiful wife and by his own admission a great marriage. There was just one problem: He had been a local football hero, and before he was married, lots of girls had thrown themselves at him. He'd had sex with some of them, and now, years later, these encounters kept coming back to him. He had tears in his eyes as he told me that when he had sex with his wife he would have flashbacks of some of the other sexual things he had done with other women. He hated it, but he could not stop the process. He had fed the experiences into his memory, and these memories were resurfacing.

What's more, much of the rush he got from sex before he was married was based on the illicitness of it. It was exciting to be pursued by a woman he hardly knew and to have women wanting to fling themselves at him. Of course, now that he was a stable married Christian man, he wanted to be sexually intimate only with his wife. But sometimes sex with his wife was not as thrilling as some of his other encounters. Sometimes married sex felt flat and boring by contrast, not because it is in fact, but because he had conditioned his responses to consider that which is forbidden to be the exciting thing.

This man had put an unnecessary burden on both himself and his wife. Sex is a very intimate and delicate act, and it should never have to be thought of in terms of "Am I enjoying this better than with the last woman or man?" Creating the circumstances for comparisons in sexual relationships is destructive and hurtful in a marriage.

We do not need these weights in our marriage. God has created logical, loving limits for us. Think of a river. Rivers are beautiful. You can sit on the banks of a river and picnic or read a book. You can go boating on a river or photograph it. Now a river has banks, but we don't see people out with placards saying "Free the river" or "Every river has the right to flow wherever it wants" or "Down with riverbanks." When a river flows within its banks, it brings harmony and order, tranquillity and peace. If the banks are taken away, the river will flood. When a river floods, we suddenly see that the reason for the banks was not to restrict the river at all but to give it limits. The banks make the river beautiful and useful. Without them, the river becomes a destructive and raging force. The same is true of sexuality. God made it to have banks and to travel within a channel. When we flow within those banks, our sexuality is peaceful, useful, and fulfilling. When we flow outside those banks, we bring destruction and havoc on ourselves and many other people around us.

Chapter Nine

HOW FAR IS TOO FAR?

Whenever I speak about relationships, people come up to talk to me afterwards and ask questions. Invariably someone will want to know what things he or she is allowed to do in the area of relationships. Is it okay to kiss? If so, how often? And with whom? And for how long?

It would seem at first glance that the Bible is almost silent on such issues. It's quite clear on the fact that we shouldn't fornicate, but what about almost fornicating? Is that wrong? What about necking and petting? It doesn't seem like the Bible even addresses this. In fact, the Bible tells us that we can do whatever we like!

> "Everything is permissible for me"—but not everything is beneficial. "Everything is permissible for me"—but I will not be mastered by anything. (1 Corinthians 6:12)

We can do anything we want, but not everything is profitable or logical or wise. Some things will not help us in the end. For instance, there is no law in the United States that says I cannot pour gasoline on my house plants. I don't do it, however, because it wouldn't be smart. It would make no sense to do it, because all I would do is kill my house plants.

Later in the same letter to the Corinthians Paul repeats himself, only this time he says:

> "Everything is permissible"—but not everything is beneficial. "Everything is permissible"—but not everything is constructive. Nobody should seek his own good, but the good of others. (1 Corinthians 10:23–24)

Again Paul is saying we can do anything we want, but not everything is loving. Not everything is for our highest good or the highest good of others.

WE NEED TO EVALUATE ALL WE DO ACCORDING TO THREE SIMPLE QUESTIONS: IS IT RIGHT? IS IT LOVING? IS IT WISE?

This is how God operates. He says you can do anything you want, but some things are stupid, some things are selfish, some things are destructive and wrong. And that is our standard for how to behave. We need to evaluate all we do according to three simple questions: Is it right? Is it loving? Is it wise?

Everything God requires of us will fall within these criteria. To help keep us within His criteria, God has given us a double alarm system of our mind and our heart. If we listen to them both, we will not make mistakes. We will stay within God's logical and loving rules.

Notice how God has written His book. In His great infinite wisdom, He has not said things like: don't kiss, don't date, do date, don't touch her there. Why? Because He wants His Word to apply in every culture, every generation, and every unique circumstance. We can always find loop holes in legalism. Therefore, God appeals to motive. His Word lays out some very clear guidelines for us on what is right, what is loving, and what is wise. The problem is, these guidelines are buried in long, seldom used words that we skim over when we read our Bible. It's time to take a serious look at some of these words and find out what God is saying to us.

If we don't know what these words mean, they cannot convict our hearts. We have our morning Bible reading, and when we read a word like *lasciviousness* we think to ourselves, I can't possibly be doing anything with a name that long. We seldom stop and think about the definitions of the words we are reading. So I am going to lay out some definitions for you. The verses below are quoted from the King James Version of the Bible, so don't worry if your Bible uses words other than the ones quoted in the King James Version; the meaning will be the same. To get at the full meaning of a word, I will refer back to the word as it is used in ancient Greek, the language the New Testament was originally written in.

LASCIVIOUSNESS

Now the works of the flesh are manifest, which are these; Adultery, fornication, uncleanness, lasciviousness. (Galatians 5:19 KJV)

And lest, when I come again, my God will humble me among you, and that I shall bewail many which have sinned already, and have not repented of the uncleanness and fornication and lasciviousness which they have committed. (2 Corinthians 12:21; see also I Peter 4:3; Jude 4 KJV)

Lasciviousness is a sin, and some reading this book have been lascivious and don't even know it. Yet the Bible says it is something that will bar us from entering the Kingdom of God. Lasciviousness can be defined as "stirring up within us, or within another person, desires that cannot be righteously satisfied." In other words, if I stir up sexual feelings in my wife, there is nothing wrong with that because it can be followed to its conclusion within the limits of a righteous relationship. However, if a single or a married person stirs up desires within another person that cannot be gratified within the limits God has placed on us, he or she is lascivious.

We can stir up sexual desires by touching someone or looking at someone in a suggestive way. Wearing revealing clothes, walking in a certain way, dancing a certain way, and saying things with a double meaning can all count as lascivious behavior if they are done to stir up sexual desire that cannot be fulfilled in ourselves or another person. The key here is intention. You can be a doctor and examine someone during his or her physical examination, or you can work in an unlicensed massage parlor and massage someone to stir him into sexual activity with you. In both cases, your hands might be in the same place, but your intention is a whole lot different.

Lasciviousness is further defined as excess, too much, or having no limits. Here it can be interchanged with the word *licentious*, which means unrestrained. This means going too far. If you are a Christian and the only thing that stops you from going too far sexually with another person is the fact that you might be caught or you're in the wrong setting or you haven't yet found someone who turns you on enough, you are a lascivious person. There are a lot of people who are not actually doing these things, but they would if they could. They might not consciously think this, but one day they get into a situation and follow through. They end up doing something they never thought they were capable of doing. So why are they surprised by their actions? They are surprised because they did not have limits set up in their heart beforehand. When we are in the backseat of the car with another person, it is not the right time to decide how far we will go.

Another dictionary meaning of the word *lasciviousness* is a catch phrase defined as "letting yourself go." Let it all hang out. Let your love flow. But Christians are never to let themselves go. They are people who take deliberate steps in accordance with the Word of God. It takes only a few wrong steps to alter our whole future, so we must set our limits now. See how much more clever it is of God to say "don't be lascivious," than to say "don't wear a two-piece swimming suit," "don't touch that," "only wink at your wife."

CONCUPISCENCE

> But sin, taking occasion by the commandment, wrought
> in me all manner of concupiscence. For without the law sin
> was dead. (Romans 7:8 KJV)

> Mortify therefore your members which are upon the earth;
> fornication, uncleanness, inordinate affection, evil concupis-
> cence, and covetousness, which is idolatry. (Colossians 3:5;
> see also 1 Thessalonians 4:3–5 KJV)

Have you been concupiscent lately? How would you know?
Well, concupiscence is a strong, abnormal sexual desire or
appetite. A concupiscent person is someone hung up on or preoccupied with sex or romance. As human beings, the first thing
we think is, "Well, who is going to say what is abnormal? I just
happen to be an oversexed individual. I have needs and desires
other people don't have." But that's just an excuse, one we've all
used at some time or another to justify thoughts or actions that
were unrighteous. What we are really saying when we rationalize this way is, "God, You gave me something that's too big for
me to handle, something that overpowers my ability to follow
You and Your Word." But that is a lie. There is nothing on Earth
that is so big it overshadows a person's ability to follow God.
Sexual behavior is a choice we make.

So what does it mean to be preoccupied? Isn't being preoccupied different for everyone? Who says my idea of what it
means to be preoccupied is right? Let me illustrate. Suppose you
and I were friends and I made a confession to you. I confessed
that whenever I was not deliberately concentrating on something, my mind immediately began to be consumed with
thoughts of marshmallows. It was as if my mind had an auto-
matic default mechanism inside it. Every day my mind would fix-
ate on marshmallows. I would spend hours each day thinking
about them. The only jokes I laughed at were marshmallow
jokes. Every time I saw a packet of marshmallows I got sweaty
palms and my heart began to race. I bought books featuring
glossy foldout color pictures of marshmallows. Whenever I

looked at these books, my eyes bugged out and I began quivering uncontrollably.

If I confessed this, you would probably think, "This guy has a real problem with marshmallows!" You wouldn't waste time trying to figure out whether this is abnormal; it would be obvious to you it was! Whether I had this kind of problem with pianos or carpets or marshmallows, you'd instantly recognize that I had a real problem.

IF WE ARE DRIVEN BY THE IDEA THAT WE MUST HAVE A GIRLFRIEND OR A BOYFRIEND, AND IF WE THINK BY THE HOUR ABOUT SEX, WE'RE CONCUPISCENT.

So how about if I put that much time and effort into thinking about sex or the opposite sex? Millions of people do. Do they have any less of a problem? I don't think so.

If we are driven by the idea that we must have a girlfriend or a boyfriend, and if we think by the hour about sex, we're concupiscent. If we find ourselves in this situation, we must be honest and admit we are preoccupied with sex. Then we must go to God and get free. We can start by telling Him we want to enjoy relationships with people without our mind going down this path all day and night. Remember, Paul told us, "Everything is permissible for me—but I will not be mastered by anything." We must not let sexual desire master us. When you are controlled, you are not loving yourself. We must not let sexual desire rob us of fulfilling relationships or take up hours of our day. God wants to help us be free. Anything that drives our life, whether it is sex, food, money, or television, needs to be brought under the Lordship of Christ so that we are no longer bound by that thing. Jesus came to bring liberty!

Sensuality

> This wisdom descendeth not from above, but is earthly, sensual, devilish. (James 3:15 KJV)

> These be they who separate themselves, sensual, having not the Spirit. (Jude 19 KJV)

Sensuality is defined as the planned appeal to the physical senses for selfish gratification. The key word here is *selfish.*

We have seen in earlier chapters that God is not against pleasure. He has put pleasure triggers throughout our bodies and in our emotions. Pleasure is not sensuality unless it is selfishly motivated. This is important; if we don't understand this, we can cross over into Eastern religious thought, which tells us that a person who is experiencing pleasure is not pleasing God. This is the mentality that motivates "holy" men to lie on beds of nails and starve themselves. Of course, the complete opposite to this mentality is living totally for the senses. As Christians, our motivation in living is to please God and serve others. Feelings are fine, but they are a by-product, and not the sole aim, of being alive.

God wants us to have the feelings. He just doesn't want us to *have* to have the feelings.

Sensuality has to do with many areas besides sex. Taking drugs for pleasure is a sensual experience. Religion can even be an excuse for sensuality. We do need to experience God. Thank God emotion has returned to Christian worship. My relationship with the most powerful and loving personality in the universe ought to produce some feelings. However, sensuality is different. It is to live for pleasure as a motivation, to let yourself demand a certain feeling, be frustrated when it's not there, and judge the strength of relationship by it. God wants us to have the feelings. He just doesn't want us to *have* to have the feelings. Emotions are not the flesh, selfishness is.

I think if we were honest, we would all admit that when we're parked in a lonely spot somewhere and begin handling each other's bodies, it's for the feelings we get. That is sensuality. It is not because we love somebody so much that we want to paw his or her body. No, it is because it makes us feel good. We do it for our selfish feelings, and not for the other person's ultimate good. If we really love someone and value him or her as a child of God, we will treat that person with gentleness and respect.

DEFRAUDING

> That no man go beyond and defraud his brother in any matter: because that the Lord is the avenger of all such, as we also have forewarned you and testified. (1 Thessalonians 4:6 KJV)

Defrauding means to use, to take advantage of, to deceive, to manipulate another person by what we say and do. In modern terms it's called "leading someone on" or "setting someone up."

When we make other people believe we like them in order to gain something from them, we are defrauding them. For example, if a girl agrees to go out with a guy not because she likes him but because she wants to be seen with him or because she likes his car, she is defrauding him. If a guy dates a girl because he wants to see if he can get his hands on her body or make his buddies envious, he is defrauding her. God is not against dating, but He is against our leading a person to believe one thing while in our heart we believe quite another. In the same way, if we enter into a covenantal courtship without sufficient knowledge of who the other person is or the ultimate will of God in the matter, we could defraud that person.

When we know someone's emotions are charged towards us and we take advantage of that for personal gain, we are defrauding that person. We are not valuing the person as a human being. I trust you are beginning to see why we began this book by talking about the value of a human being. Without such understanding, everything becomes relative. But when we add human value into the equation, we have a clear directive for how to treat other people. Regrettably, we don't always clearly follow this directive. All too often, the people we get involved with romantically are the people we end up treating the worst. How many people are unable to go up to their "ex" and have a normal, civil conversation? There is something wrong when this happens. After all, the other person is more than just someone we were romantically involved with; he or she is also our neighbor. And remember, God says we are to love our neighbor as ourselves. That directive does not go out the window just because we were romantically involved with our neighbor.

The command not to defraud applies not only to singles but to married couples as well:

> Defraud ye not one the other, except it be with consent for a time, that ye may give yourselves to fasting and prayer; and come together again, that Satan tempt you not for your incontinency. (1 Corinthians 7:5 KJV)

Society often says, "You don't own me. We may be married, but I make my own decisions and do what I want. If you don't like it, that's your problem." But for married couples, this verse tells us sexuality is never to be used as a bribe or a threat. Regrettably, such use is a common occurrence in Christian marriages. A wife might say something like, "If I don't get a new couch, you won't get what you want."

The truth is, the wife doesn't have authority over her own body except by consent of her husband. Neither does the husband have authority over his body except by consent of the wife. If you don't want to be owned by another person, don't get married, because the Bible says a married couple own each other. That is why sexual abstinence in a marriage should take place only with mutual consent. Neither party can demand sex, and neither party can withhold it. This mutual freedom agreement and benefit also determines what sexual practices we engage in in marriage.

A husband defrauds his wife, or a wife defrauds her husband, whenever one demands sex without the other's consent or when one gets into a bad mood and manipulates or refuses the other. Sexuality can be a tremendously manipulative tool, and Christians, married and single, must not use it that way.

FORNICATION

Most of my life I heard that fornication was sex before marriage and adultery was sex outside of marriage. Perhaps that's what you think, too. But if we read the Scriptures, we discover that these definitions while true are not complete. About fornication, Paul writes:

> Meats for the belly, and the belly for meats: but God shall destroy both it and them. Now the body is not for fornication, but for the Lord; and the Lord for the body....Flee fornication. Every sin that a man doeth is without the body; but he that committeth fornication sinneth against his own body. (1 Corinthians 6:13, 18 KJV)

When we look up *fornication* in Greek, it is the word *porniea*. It means to indulge unlawfully or outside of God's limits. *Porniea* is also translated in the Bible as idolatry or harlotry. If the word has a familiar ring to it, it's because *porniea* is the root word of *pornography*, which is the study of unlawful things.

Let's think about pornography for a minute. Christians are against pornography. They picket stores that sell it and write letters to Congress about how bad it is, but when you ask exactly what is wrong with pornography, many Christians cannot answer intelligently. They sputter and stutter about it's not being right, about naked bodies being dirty, and about exploitation. And the world responds with, "What's wrong with admiring a naked body? Didn't God make the body? And besides, the woman in the photos is over twenty-one. She got well paid. She liked doing it and will do it again tomorrow."

Let me tell you why pornography is wrong. It is because pornography destroys the intimacy God created. "Miss January" was meant to be observed for the purpose of pleasure by only one person—her husband. Married couples can view each other for pleasure because it is within God's limits. But if we look at someone for sexual pleasure outside of marriage, we could be committing fornication, because it violates intimacy. So, seeing a body is not fornication (think of doctors), but dwelling on that body for sexual pleasure is. That the word *porniea* is also translated idolatry in some places suggests unlawful indulgence with thoughts, because idolatry is worshiping our mind's substitute for God rather than the real God. So sexual fantasies (a substitute for the real thing) can be fornication. Lastly *porniea* is translated harlotry, which is unlawful indulgence with our entire being, or sex outside of marriage.

IF I TAKE MY AFFECTIONS OR MY ROMANTIC ABILITY, WHICH BELONG TO MY WIFE, AND I GIVE THEM TO ANOTHER WOMAN, I'M AN ADULTERER, EVEN IF I NEVER TOUCH THE OTHER PERSON.

ADULTERY

Thou shalt not commit adultery. (Exodus 20:14 KJV)

Oddly enough, the Greek word for adultery carries no necessary sexual connotation. It comes from the same root as the word *mine*, showing ownership or belonging. Adultery means setting our affections or romantic ability on that which is not ours or on that to which we do not belong. The word *adultery* is used with regard to married people because married people belong to someone.

Here is how it works. If I take my affections or my romantic ability, which belong to my wife, and I give them to another woman, I'm an adulterer, even if I never touch the other person. Do you think that sounds extreme? Let's look back in the Old Testament.

But thou hast played the harlot with many lovers; yet return again to me, saith the LORD. (Jeremiah 3:1 KJV)

There are many times when God accused the children of Israel of playing the harlot. In saying this, He did not mean they were involved in sexual immorality, though many of them were. Rather, He was referring to the fact that they had set their hearts on other things. They had turned away from God and towards substitutes for Him.

Jesus told us:

You have heard that it was said, "Do not commit adultery." But I tell you that anyone who looks at a woman lustfully has already committed adultery with her in his heart. (Matthew 5:27 KJV)

We may have never touched someone other than our spouse, but we have turned our heart toward another with thoughts that are sexual or romantic. Jesus calls this adultery. We have wanted something for ourselves that does not belong to us. In doing so, we have crossed the line in our motives, and that is all it takes to be an adulterer. Often we excuse this as only an "emotional attachment." That's romantic attraction and it belongs to some-one else, so we could have crossed the line.

What if you are single? Is it okay to give your affections to each other? Yes, but with limits. Never act in selfishness, and never allow anyone else to take the place of God in your affections.

THE BOTTOM LINE

A friend of mine one day recently met her former live-in boyfriend on the beach. The man asked her out to dinner, but she didn't give him an immediate answer. She went home and prayed about it. Finally, she thought it would be a good opportu-nity to share the gospel with him, so she accepted his invitation.

When they had finished eating, he drove her out to a nice, lonely spot, where he parked the car and started "putting the moves" on her. She didn't scream, "Get your filthy hands off me!" Instead, she very calmly said, "Look, I just want you to know that since I have given my life to God, my body is now the temple of the Holy Spirit."

Even though the man wasn't a Christian, he understood how important her faith was to her. He never touched her again. She stood up for her values, and he respected her for it!

The young woman wasn't using religious double-talk just to fend off an overaggressive pass. She realized her true value to God and insisted that her body be treated with the respect and value due a temple of the Holy Spirit.

That young woman provides a perfect example of the attitude we need to have when determining what we can and cannot do in our dating lives. We must keep in mind that our bodies are the temple of the Holy Spirit. We need to treat our bodies, and those of the people we date, with the respect due the dwelling place of the Spirit of God!

If we are honest with ourselves as we read through these Bible definitions of relational sin, we will find plenty of guidelines. Our problem is that we often ask the wrong question. Instead of wanting to know how far we can go, we ought to be asking, "Is what I'm doing or want to do the most loving thing I could do towards God, towards my neighbor, and towards myself?"

Paul sums this up well when he says:

> So whether you eat or drink or whatever you do, do it all for the glory of God. (1 Corinthians 10:31)

And this includes dating for the glory of God!

WALLS OF PROTECTION

Some of the oldest Bible stories have the most to tell us about God's dealings with men and women. Take, for example, the story of Isaac's marriage to Rebekah.

Abraham had a son named Isaac. He decided it was time for his son to find himself a wife, move out from under his father's covering, and create a family unit of his own. So he talked to Isaac, and as it turned out, Isaac was eager to find a wife. But how was he going to do this? Isaac knew all of the local girls, and for one reason or another, they were not right for him. So where was he going to find a wife?

Abraham called the family servant and charged him with finding the right woman for Isaac. So the family servant harnessed up ten camels and set out to find Isaac a wife. Notice that no one seemed worried that the servant would come back with the wrong woman. They all trusted God to lead the servant to just the right person: a woman who would appeal to Isaac in every way, including sexually.

The family servant set out, and eventually he spied a town in the distance. As he approached the town, God spoke to him and said, "A local woman will come to the well and offer to draw water for your camels. She is the one I have in mind for Isaac. Go back to her house with her and meet her family."

So the servant found the town well and waited there. Several beautiful young women were there, and the servant's heart raced. Was one of these women to be Isaac's wife? But they all went about their own business, drawing water for their needs. Not one of them took any notice of the stranger at the well.

Then another woman arrived. She, too, was beautiful. She was singing softly to herself. As soon as she saw the stranger, she approached him and offered to draw water for his camels.

Abraham's servant was delighted. He knew God had gone before him and picked this special woman for Isaac. He thanked her for her offer to draw water for his camels and asked if he could go home with her to meet her parents.

Rebekah, as the woman was named, nodded in agreement. After the servant met Rebekah's parents, it was soon settled. Rebekah would accompany the servant back across the desert to Abraham's land. Isaac was out tilling a field when he saw them approaching. Genesis 24:67 records that "Isaac brought her into the tent...and he married Rebekah. So she became his wife, and he loved her." Rebekah, too, was probably hearing from God about a husband and was likely instructed to offer water for the camels, knowing that this man would take her to God's best for her.

SHOULD MEN WHO WANT A WIFE HANG OUT AT GAS STATIONS READY TO MARRY THE FIRST WOMAN WHO OFFERS TO PUMP GAS FOR THEM?

So why did I tell you this story? Should men who want a wife hang out at gas stations ready to marry the first woman who offers to pump gas for them? I don't think so. The point is not that Rebekah drew water for the camels but that God was interested in the relationship between Isaac and Rebekah from the very beginning. He knew both of them, and He orchestrated the perfect timing for them to separate from their families and come together. God knew Isaac would find Rebekah physically attractive, and vice versa. The rest is detail—detail that changes from culture to culture and generation to generation—but the principles remains the same: First, the God who made us with our attraction gift knows how to lead us to someone who will fulfill all our desires. I am often asked what I think of Christians dating. Is it right, or is it wrong? Quite honestly, I don't think God cares whether we date or don't date. Today I don't think God is into arranged marriages either. Any system will fail if we are selfish, and almost any system will work if we follow right principles.

Second, good decisions in life come from good relationships in family and community. This is the reason God created the family unit and other aspects of community life. It is also the reason Satan is working overtime to split them up. The Isaac and Rebekah story helps to illustrate the reason for family.

In God's ideal situation for families, there is one woman and one man producing a child. The mother and the father love each other and submit to each other. They also love God and encourage the other to walk with the Lord. When a child is added to their union, they love the child and teach the child to love God. The child in turn loves his or her parents and submits to them. The parents direct the child and help him or her to make the right choices in life.

This is why God starts all human beings out as babies. Human babies are the most dependent beings on Earth. Without parents to feed them, carry them, and protect them, they will not survive. God did this for a purpose—so that we would learn a pattern of submission and dependence so that when we got older, we would be able to use the same model of submission and dependence to relate to God Himself.

The parents' protection and love produces security in the child, and a child who is secure is free to develop a whole personality and tends to have right direction and values in life. The family is crucial to this process. Society, on the other hand, tries to tell us that a family doesn't really matter, that any group of people living under the same roof is a family. But this simply is not true. A family is a group of people spiritually joined within a protective circle created by God as they have submitted to the biblical truth of marriage.

IN GOD'S PLAN A CHILD COMES OUT FROM THE PROTECTIVE CIRCLE OF HIS OR HER FAMILY ONLY TO MAKE ANOTHER CIRCLE.

In God's plan a child comes out from the protective circle of his or her family only to make another circle:

> Therefore shall a man leave his father and mother, and shall cleave unto his wife: and they shall be one flesh. (Genesis 2:24 KJV)

For this cause (only) shall a man leave father and mother, to cleave to a wife. This command of God says both that marriage is the only reason for leaving a family and that when we marry we are to leave—in other words be bordered off into another authority structure. This new circle is a family of its own. When children are born, they are in this circle of protection provided by the parents' marriage commitment to each other.

This circle of protection is why the devil cannot possess a baby. Babies are powerless, yet the devil has no access to them. Why? Because babies are born into a circle of protection. Of course, the devil does not like this. It puts him in the same situation he was in at the Garden of Eden. He was an onlooker with no access to the people there, at least until they broke down the protective wall. Today the devil is hell-bent on destroying families and breaking down the wall of protection. Once that wall has been breached, he can come in and create havoc in the lives of the people who have become vulnerable to his attack.

Exactly how does the devil break down this protective wall formed by the circle of intimacy, love, and mutual submission that should surround a family?

First and most obviously, he breaks down families through separation and divorce. Whether we're single or married right now, the devil is going to attack our marriage. It doesn't matter how "made in heaven" a marriage is or how compatible or in love we are, the enemy seeks to bring disunity. If he can incite enough strife and independent attitude, it gives him influence in the circle.

ONLY THE TWO PEOPLE IN A MARRIAGE CAN ULTIMATELY DESTROY THE MARRIAGE.

I'm not saying the devil alone can destroy our marriage; we have to cooperate with him to do that. Only the two people in a marriage can ultimately destroy the marriage. However, the devil has strategies to encourage the breakup of every marriage. This breakup does not have to be just a physical separation. Even within a marriage, a breakdown of intimacy and trust can lead to people living under the same roof but "doing their own thing." Sometimes this occurs so subtly that people outside the family may not even notice. Only those within the family know whether or not the couple are united in their hearts and intentions.

There comes a point in the break down that we are "putting asunder what God has joined together," leaving a hole in the protective wall around our marriage. Everyone involved, including the children, becomes vulnerable. Many of us have probably heard a couple who are about to divorce say something like, "We have kept things very civilized in front of the children. It should hardly affect them at all. We're going to take turns with them at holidays and the like, and we have promised never to say anything negative about each other to them. It's our divorce, and the children don't need to be involved in it."

This attitude shows a lack of understanding of what effect divorce can have.

IF WE NEGLECT TO NURTURE RELATIONSHIPS WITHIN THE PROTECTIVE CIRCLE OF THE FAMILY, WE CREATE THE CONDITIONS FOR THE WALL TO BE BREACHED.

Second, even if a couple hasn't separated or divorced, neglect can produce a hole in the wall. Part of loving a child involves spending time affirming the child, letting the child know in a variety of ways that he or she is loved. If we neglect to nurture relationships within the protective circle of the family, we create the conditions for the wall to be breached.

People sometimes ask me why I don't spend time warning teenagers of the dangers of unprotected sex. They say, "You must warn them that they could get AIDS and die." But these people don't get it. I talk to young people nearly every week who say to me, "I don't care if I die. I just want to do it, and nothing is going to stop me." This reflects an attitude of self-hatred and despair that typically comes from neglect.

Third, rebellion will punch a hole in the wall more surely than just about anything else. Satan himself was the first being ever to rebel, and he delights in promoting rebellion here on earth.

When a person rebels they are saying, "I am not under them! I want to be my own person, do my own thing, when and if I want to!"

It is vital to remember that when we cooperate with the devil in these three key areas, we greatly assist him in tearing down the walls of protection God has built around us and our family relationships. Next, to protect ourselves and those we date, we will establish the principles of a loving, effective dating philosophy.

Chapter Eleven

A DATING PHILOSOPHY

*D*amaging another human being is never an act of love, yet more people are damaged through dating than possibly anything else. Christian young people routinely deeply hurt each other in the name of love. The hurts from broken relationships are often deep and permanent.

CHRISTIAN YOUNG PEOPLE ROUTINELY DEEPLY HURT EACH OTHER IN THE NAME OF LOVE.

Go to any old-folks home in the country, and I guarantee you will find people in their seventies and eighties who can tell you about breaking up with a girlfriend or boyfriend when they were in their twenties. They talk about it as though it were yesterday. Often the pain of the breakup is still visible on their faces.

Perhaps you've experienced a difficult breakup yourself. You may feel as if you've endured a mortal blow, and all the while your parents are patting you on the hand and telling you, "Don't worry, there are plenty more fish in the sea. Maybe this was just an infatuation. Try concentrating on something else to snap you out of it."

Parents and others around us often don't understand how deeply a breakup can affect a person. The hurt from a breakup can last a lifetime. When a relationship begins, it starts with two people minding their own business. Then the attraction gift kicks in, and they begin to develop feelings for each other. Next, they start to tell each other how they feel, and bingo, they are linked to each other, and breaking up becomes very hard to do.

Let's look at what is happening behind the scenes here. These two people have expressed their feelings. We tend to underestimate the power of the spoken word. The Bible tells us, though, that when we confess with our mouths and believe in our hearts, we will be saved. The act of confessing, or saying what we are thinking, is powerful enough to get us saved, and it is certainly powerful enough to get us into a lot of trouble in a relationship!

EACH TIME WE TELL SOMEONE WE LOVE HIM OR HER AND OUR HEART IS DIRECTED TOWARD THAT PERSON, WE TIE A CORD AROUND THE BOTH OF US.

So the couple confess their love for, dependence on, and admiration for each other. This, along with a second factor, that of projecting their hearts towards each other, produces a powerful bond.

Each time we tell someone we love him or her and our heart is directed toward that person, we tie a cord around the both of us. The more we do this, the more cords that tie us together, and the more painful it is to break them. What we say to a person whose heart is charged towards us is tremendously significant to that person. It creates another link between us. When we say, "You're the neatest person I have ever been with," the words are simple, but they create a chord that binds us together.

Kissing and hugging and even holding hands communicates something. The first thing we think of when someone reaches out to hold our hand is, what does he or she mean by this? Every time we communicate with another person, either by an action or by a word, we create a bond with that person. I'm not saying that this is wrong. Neither am I talking about sexual sin here, or any other type of sin. I am merely saying that this is the reality of what happens when our heart is exposed to another person and the other person's heart is exposed to us.

All too often, I have guys say to me, "I don't get what the big deal is. Sure we hugged and kissed and stuff, but I never told her I loved her. I don't know why she's so upset that I haven't called her for a month."

Going out with a person means something in our society. Holding hands means something. Kissing a person means something. If we're in a relationship where our hearts are directed towards each other and words and actions of affection have been shared, these things mean something. Our emotions are exposed as a result.

The best example of this that I can think of happened when I was ten years old. I was at a baseball game, standing in the front row to get a good view of what was happening. The batter struck out, and in his anger he hurled the bat behind him. Guess what? It hit me right in the mouth. A surge of unbelievable pain shot through my body. All I could think of was getting home. I ran out the gate and down the street. By the time I got home, my shirt was soaked with blood and I was ready to pass out from the pain. I found my mother, and she looked in my mouth. She went white and rushed off to call the dentist. I wondered what she had seen, so I looked in the bathroom mirror myself. Half of my left front tooth was missing. It had been sheered off diagonally, leaving what looked like a fang. I was fascinated by the way I looked.

As I peered more closely I could see tiny white threads dangling out of the tooth. With a shock that made me sit down, I realized those threads were nerves dangling in the open air. No wonder the pain was so agonizing.

The reason I felt so much pain was that the nerve, which normally causes no pain when bound up inside my tooth, extended into a realm it was never designed to be in. A tooth nerve was never meant to dangle freely in the air. You can take my word for that!

When a relationship breaks up, the emotions we extended towards the other person are left dangling in midair. They were never meant to be exposed like that. They were made to be sur-rounded by a committed relationship. So when that relationship is over, the person is in tremendous emotional pain. God designed us so that when we extend our feelings towards another person, they are to be embraced by that person.

Of course, we live in a less than ideal world, and it is not always possible to feel attracted to a person who is attracted to us or be as committed as the other person is committed to us. So how can we decrease the probability of being hurt in a relation-ship as well as lessen the intensity of the emotional pain if we are hurt?

WE MUST HAVE A
DATING PHILOSOPHY.

To do this, we must have a dating philosophy. Without pre-determined principles, we are destined to make mistakes that will hurt both ourselves and others. It's no good just telling our-selves we'll get into a relationship and "see what happens." Believe me, "it" happens! We need some principles beforehand to make sure that things don't happen in a way that causes us deep emotional pain. We need to promise ourselves right now that we're not going to get into another relationship, or get any deeper into the one we may already be in, until we have a clear understanding of how to proceed.

PRINCIPLE ONE: GET YOUR MOTIVES RIGHT

This principle will cut out a lot of dating right away. We should not be dating because everyone else has a boyfriend or girlfriend and we'll feel stupid if we don't have one, too. Single people feel great pressure to be dating. They feel like a reject if they don't date. Even in churches we perpetuate this dating syndrome. We arrange youth-group dances and Valentine's dinners instead of hayrides and sports games where young people can get to know each other free from the stress of feeling they need to arrive with a partner.

When we arrange such events as dances and dinners, we send young people the message, "If you're datable, you're somebody." So these young people go out, not really caring about who they're going out with as long as they have a date. They end up going out with people they don't like to places they don't want to go, just because they feel they have to date. They think, "I am, therefore I date." But a person who must have a boyfriend or a girlfriend at all times is insecure. Period. I'd rather be respected as a human being than be just a date for someone, wouldn't you?

When we pursue relationships for our own reasons, we can often miss what God has planned for us. What happens if we're tied up in a relationship that is going nowhere and someone who would be God's choice for us comes on the scene? Are we going to be free to pursue the person? I don't think so.

Likewise, any person we date is a valuable human being. The person is created and loved by God. Whether or not we continue in a relationship with the person, we should always be concerned about that person's highest good. It saddens me to think that some of the worst relationships in youth groups and churches are between people who used to date each other. How can this be? One day these two people are saying all the things they admire about each other; the next day they're trashing each other to their friends after prayer meeting. This ought not be. Christians, especially those who date each other, need to be careful to follow the golden rule and treat the other person the way they themselves want to be treated.

Wondering how far we can get the other person to go is also a bad motive. If our purpose to date is to handle someone else's body, we'd better not date until we have worked through our problem. We will only damage ourselves and others if we proceed with this motive.

There is only one appropriate motive for Christian dating, and that is to get to know another person so that we can enhance that person's life while honoring God, honoring the person, and honoring ourselves. If we cannot do this, we dare not date until we can.

PRINCIPLE TWO: DETERMINE TO BE A REAL PERSON, NOT JUST A PROJECTION

So many relationships are not real at all. They are simply two people projecting the best about themselves and interacting with each other's projection. But a relationship based on a projection will never lead to a happy marriage, because in marriage we have to deal with the whole person in every situation and not just what the other person wants us to see.

Once I dated a girl for two years. It was during the 1960s when girls all wore their hair teased up and cemented in place with gobs of hairspray. One day I arrived early to pick the girl up for a date. As I stood in the hallway waiting for her, a girl brushed past. She had obviously just showered and was wearing a robe. Her hair hung limply over her shoulders. She looked pale, and I nodded to her as she scurried off. It wasn't until later that night that my girlfriend told me she was the one in the robe. Imagine that! I had dated her for two years and didn't recognize her when she wasn't all primped up and ready to go on a date! That experience scared me and got me thinking about just how well you could really get to know someone in a dating context.

I think it is unrealistic to be opposed to dating, but we need to be very careful before we get into a relationship. I believe the dating culture has produced the divorce culture. How? As a society we've become so used to splitting up when things get a little difficult. In my generation, when we said, "We broke up," we were referring to a dating relationship that was over. In this generation we say, "We broke up," just as casually to refer to a marriage breaking up. We have trivialized dating, and now we're trivializing marriage. This easy-in/easy-out approach to relationships and marriage is a slippery slope. We must watch that we don't develop bad habits in our dating that we could unwittingly carry over into marriage with disastrous consequences. We must choose to treat people in a loving way, and even if we stop dating someone, to still be committed to that person's highest good. The one we were dating is a valuable person.

PRINCIPLE THREE: GIVE UP YOUR RIGHTS TO SEX AND MARRIAGE

What am I implying here? Do I mean that sex and marriage are on a lower spiritual plane? Do I mean that if we're really spiritual we will never need sex or marriage and instead consider ourselves married to Jesus? The answer is absolutely not. Such thinking is a perversion of God's truth. God created two sexes. He invented our sexuality. Therefore, it is not a lower calling to use what God has given us. What I'm talking about here is the attitude that we've developed that basically says, "I'm not a monk. I'm not a nun. I'm not the single type. I *have* to have a partner."

SEX IS NOT A BASIC NEED, IT'S A BASIC FUNCTION, AND THAT IS ENTIRELY DIFFERENT FROM A NEED.

Often we adopt this attitude because we don't want others to think we have no sex drive. So we say, "I don't know about you, but I sure need to be married," and we smile and wink. But as Christians, we don't need anything other than what God gives us. And if we give up our rights to dating and marriage, God can give them back to us as a gift, in His time and in His way.

To be free in the dating realm, we need to give up our rights to sex and marriage. If we don't, the search for sex will consume us. Now, giving up the right to sex is hard for most people. In our pride we feel like we're oversexed and just cannot go without sex. We might even believe that if we go too long without sexual involvement we'll go crazy. We think we need an outlet—that we're going to do something wild unless we release our sexual tension.

This way of thinking is an easy trap to fall into. I have been there myself. I used to teach that sex is a biological need, like water, air, and food. Now I look back and wonder how I could have taught that. There is a fundamental difference between sex and water, air, and food. Without water we will die. Without air we will die. Without food we will die. But a lack of sex has never killed a single person! Sex is not a basic need, it's a basic function, and that is entirely different from a need. If we think that sex is a basic biological need, it will drive us every day of our life, even if we're married. Not only this, but if we think it is a need, we rationalize that we have a right to it. We do whatever it takes to eat and drink and breathe, and if we put sex in the same category, we'll do whatever it takes to get sex as well. But we need to understand that sexual activity is optional for a human being. We can live with it, and we can live without it. Many people go through their lives without being sexually active. Of course, doing so is totally foreign to the way our society thinks.

ONLY GOD KNOWS HOW MANY OPPORTUNITIES FOR USEFUL SERVICE HAVE BEEN SQUANDERED BY YOUNG PEOPLE WHO SPENT MOST OF THEIR ENERGY LOOKING FOR A PARTNER.

None of us can dictate to God the gifts He will give to us and when He will give them. What is the point of spending our lives trying to manipulate God into finding us a spouse? Think of any married person you know. He or she is only a minute away from being single. A heart can stop, a gun can go off, a car can crash. The Bible tells us our times are in God's hands, and it is foolish to try to strong-arm Him into complying with our wishes. For every person who says, "I waited too long to get married," there are a hundred or more who say, "I wish I'd waited longer." God's time frame will not be rushed.

If we think we have a right to be married, it will dominate our thinking. Every time we're in a group we will be looking over our shoulder thinking, "I wonder if my future husband or wife is here. I wonder if he or she is in this church? I wonder if I should go on this particular mission trip, or if there's more chance of meeting a girl or boy on that one." I've seen young people whose whole motivation in life has been to find the person they're "supposed" to marry. What a waste of the energy and precious time God has given us. Our teens and twenties can be some of our most productive years. They can set us up in a career, get us started on our education, or expose us to missionary opportunities. Only God knows how many opportunities for useful service have been squandered by young people who spent most of their energy looking for a partner.

The key is to give our desires back to God, to give up what we think are our rights, and trust the Lord to do the best thing for us. Remember, God is in favor of marriage, sex, and families. He is not waiting for us to give Him our desires so He can send us to Africa to live an old maid's existence! No. God does not want to take things away from us. God is for us; He will not take advantage of us. It's okay to say, "Lord, lead me to a person who would be good for me and I for her," and then leave it with Him and go on with everything else He has for you.

The Act of Sex

Sex was designed by God to be an overflow of the love and intimacy two people have for each other within a marriage. In many ways, sex is like adult baptism or communion. It may be shocking for some to hear me say this, so let me explain. Both baptism and communion are prefaced upon the person receiving them having a relationship with Jesus Christ. Having this relationship with Christ means that getting baptized is a powerful, life-changing event. In baptism, we commit our life to Christ and ask Him to wash away our sins. When we come up out of the water, we feel fresh and clean before God. Or consider communion. When a Christian takes communion, he is entering into oneness with a holy God. I've seen people healed and delivered just through the act of communion.

But what if a person who is not saved gets baptized or takes communion? Simple. Baptism will get him wet, and communion will give him a tiny wafer or sliver of bread to eat and a sip of wine or grape juice, nothing more. A non-Christian would wonder what all the fuss is about. Why? Because the acts of baptism and communion are symbols of something much more significant that has happened within a person. They are an outward manifestation of an inward attitude. And that's the way in which baptism and communion are like sex.

Sex is an outward manifestation of an inward reality. The sexual act makes you about as physically open and vulnerable as a person can get. After all, you take off all your clothes and get so close to the other person that your bodies merge. You can't get any closer than that! Yet I counsel young married women all the time who say, "I don't feel loved." And their husband says, "What do you mean? I love you every night!" Then the wife explains that's not what she means.

What is happening here? To the husband the sexual act is how he expresses love to his wife. But she is telling him she doesn't feel loved, even though the couple engages in sex. Why is this? It is because sex is a symbol of openness and intimacy. You cannot get from the outward act to the inward attitude. Rather, it's the other way around. Those who do not have genuine openness and intimacy with their partner will wonder what the big deal is. One marriage partner cannot make the other's "sexual" cup overflow unless he or she has a heart that is committed to that partner. People intuitively know that sex is somehow supposed to be more than it actually is for them, so they do all sorts of things to try to enhance it. They do it in groups or after drinking alcohol or taking other drugs, or they do acrobatics and use props. Deep inside they keep looking for more. But their antics will never fill the cup because the filling has to start from within.

It doesn't matter how many times a nonbeliever gets baptized, it will not induce feelings of repentance and love for Jesus in the person. And if the nonbeliever drinks enough communion wine and eats enough wafers, it will still not give him a sense of real communion with Jesus. So why do we think that repeatedly having sex will bring more closeness with our partner? In fact, the opposite is true. If I baptized someone over and over again in the sincere hope that the person would accept Jesus, in the end the person would despise me and the whole process of baptism. The person may well think the that whole thing is a hoax. In the same way, if sex is not a reflection of an inner attitude of commitment and love towards our partner, then our partner will eventually come to despise performing the sex act itself with us.

I hear about this all the time. Wives say, "I love my husband, and I want to please him, but I just recoil inside when he touches me." There is no significant communication or listening within such a relationship. The husband has made an idol out of the outward symbol rather than pursuing the real treasure of openness and intimacy.

Let's face it, if sex could create an environment for intimacy and commitment, prostitutes would be the most loving, caring, empathetic, committed people on earth. But they're not. Emotional intimacy and commitment create the environment for sexual fulfillment, not the other way around.

Principle Four: Take Time to Develop Nonromantic Relationships

Society sets a trap for young people. Even as preteens, many boys and girls are encouraged to think in terms of who their girlfriend or boyfriend is. What a crazy thing to do. The goal for our children and ourselves should be to develop a wide range of interesting and deep friendships with members of the opposite sex.

GOD DESIGNED US TO HAVE A WIDE RANGE OF RELATIONSHIPS WITH A WIDE RANGE OF PEOPLE.

Just think of it. Half the world is made up of people who are a different sex from us! If from a young age we're taught to categorize each person in terms of "possibilities," we are devaluing half the human race. God designed us to have a wide range of relationships with a wide range of people. So many young people lose sight of this, though. A girl identifies a boy who is a possibility and interacts with him only. He becomes her boyfriend. A boy does the same with a girl, who becomes his girlfriend. But what happens when a couple who have related this way get married? Both of them know how to relate to the opposite sex only in terms of sizing the other up to see if that person is a romantic possibility. Now that they are married, they cannot look for romantic possibilities, so they have no way to relate to anyone of the opposite sex. At work, at church, and in social contexts, they meet people of the opposite sex but don't know what to talk to them about. They don't know what they might be interested in or how to get to know them better. In fixating on romantic possibilities as a young person and relating only to those people, they have ripped themselves off. A certain freedom and balance come with being able to develop deep and meaningful relationships with members of both sexes.

When a person is single, it is much healthier to develop nonromantic relationships with others in an authentic, relaxed way. From there, a romantic relationship can emerge. In this way, two people begin their romantic relationship as friends who already know a lot about each other.

It is very difficult to go about things in the reverse order. I learned this lesson when I was going to college. Much to my surprise, I found I was closer to several of my friends' girlfriends than my friends were. These girls would take me aside and say, "Dean,

I need someone to talk to, and I think I can talk to you. I can't talk to my boyfriend." I began to realize I had deeper relationships with these girls than their romantic partners had, and it scared me. I began to see the weakness of jumping from one relationship to the next, as if romantic relationships were the way to form deep and lasting friendships.

Having a group of friends is much healthier and less complicated. It is better to be with the opposite sex in a context where there is no tension or awkwardness. Then, when you do get romantically involved with someone, you end up marrying a friend rather than a date.

"Hey, I'm full of lust. I lie a lot. I have a bad temper, and I steal when I really want something. Do you want to go out with me?"

Principle Five: Get Yourself Free from Sin and Straightened Out

You wouldn't dream of saying to someone, "Hey, I'm full of lust. I lie a lot. I have a bad temper, and I steal when I really want something. Do you want to go out with me?" Yet in reality, Christians impose upon each other like this all the time.

To avoid doing this, we need to get ourselves free from sin and hang-ups before we do any more dating. We are not ready to date until we're free from moodiness, manipulation, and game playing. In fact, if we are not free from these things, we are not worth dating, and certainly not worth marrying. We must become secure in the Lord. Otherwise the type of person who is attracted to us will not be the type of person we want to be married to.

Many Christians have hang-ups and bad habits they need to straighten out, but instead of going to the cross and becoming a whole person, they spend their time searching for a girlfriend or a boyfriend to make themselves complete. How is this loving to the person we intend to "inflict" ourselves upon? Until we are a whole person in Christ Jesus, we have no business dating anyone. Period.

I was in a relationship with a young woman once when I was very insecure. I doubted that poor woman's love for me over and over until she would break down and cry in frustration. Looking back, I know I had no business being in any romantic relationship at that time in my life. I simply was not secure enough in who I was to be any kind of romantic partner to another person. I ended up hurting the woman and wasting a lot of time that I could have spent getting myself together as a Christian. Later, I apologized for the way I had treated her, but it would have been a lot more loving for both of us if I had not dated her in the first place.

EACH OF US PASSES THROUGH THREE PHASES BETWEEN BIRTH AND DEATH: CHILDHOOD, ADOLESCENCE, AND ADULTHOOD.

PRINCIPLE SIX: GIVE HIGHER PRIORITY TO PERSONALITY DEVELOPMENT THAN TO DATABILITY

Each of us passes through three phases between birth and death: childhood, adolescence, and adulthood. Everyone loves a baby or a little child. Adults peer into a stroller and tell the proud new parents how blessed they are to have a new baby. It's so cute when toddlers wrap their arms around their parents and give them a big squeeze. Then these precious little children reach adolescence. Suddenly, the outlook is gloomy. Other parents begin commiserating with us. "Adolescence is such a difficult age," they say. "You just have to grit your teeth and get through it somehow." Or they say, "We'll be praying for you, you'll need it. Don't expect your kid to have a meaningful conversation with you for the next five years!" They laugh as they speak, but they mean it. But when we joke like this, whose integrity are we calling into question? Who, after all, designed adolescence? God. And why did He design adolescence? He designed it as a time when a person gets to be an apprentice adult. In some ways the child is an adult, and in other ways, he or she is still a child. Adolescents don't have full responsibility for their life, but slowly, in fits and starts, they learn how to cope. Adolescence is a time for people to develop their individual personality and to discover who they really are and what it is they like and don't like.

Our character is formed in childhood, and our personalities develop during adolescence. What happens to children who are not raised in a protective, closed family circle or to children who get messed up by family problems? These children are not adequately parented, and as a result, their character is not properly formed and they cannot cope with being apprentice adults. They simply have not had the environment and preparation they need to make it as adults. When they reach adolescence, instead of seeing members of the opposite sex as interesting people to relate to, they see them as simply body parts. They spend their whole time wondering whether the other person likes them "in that way," and they never really grow up. They may even get married and have children, but they still have not learned how to relate to other people. They have not learned lessons that should have been learned in adolescence.

STAND OUTSIDE A KINDERGARTEN AND THEN STAND OUTSIDE A BAR FOR A WHILE. YOU WILL HEAR VARIATIONS OF THE SAME CONVERSATION AT BOTH!

Stand outside a kindergarten and then stand outside a bar for a while. You will hear variations of the same conversation at both! "My father has a bigger truck than yours." "My truck has new mag wheels, bet yours doesn't."

Turn on a talk show sometime if you're not convinced. Just listening to some of the conversations on these shows will convince you that many grown-ups are nothing more than adult children. Something interrupted their character development in childhood.

Many adult Christians are married children, too. They may be physically mature, but emotionally and spiritually they have a lot of growing up to do. I cannot count the number of times I've talked to wives who have said to me, "My husband was such a good football player, or had such a great body, or was continually chased by other girls, but now we're married and he doesn't talk." I ask them if he ever talked. They usually dance around the question for a minute or two and finally answer, "Well, no, I guess he didn't. I just never noticed it."

We ought not spend our adolescence preoccupied with the search for a mate. Instead, we should spend it growing up, developing our character, and learning to love the Lord more. Then, when we do get romantically involved with someone, we will be able to choose a person who, like ourselves, has a well-developed character and personality. The person will not be a full-grown baby who will be a weight on us for the rest of our life.

DETERMINE TO PLEASE GOD

We have no right as Christians to do anything that does not please God the Father. I received a letter from a young woman I once counseled who told me she was no longer walking with the Lord. She explained that she was dating a guy she knew God did not want her to date, but she would not give him up. How crazy! She had dumped the Creator of the universe for a guy with a hairy chest! We must be careful not to follow a similar path. We must determine beforehand that we will live our life to please our Lord and Savior. No man or woman is worth laying aside the privilege of pleasing and serving God.

WHEN WE ALLOW GOD TO MEET OUR NEEDS, WE CAN SAY TO OUR SPOUSE, "I AM NOT HERE BECAUSE I HAVE NEEDS. I AM HERE BECAUSE I LOVE YOU."

DETERMINE NOT TO MARRY OUT OF A SENSE OF NEED

We say, "I need you. I have so many needs, and you meet my needs." Then we marry, and all at once the other person stops meeting our needs. No human being can meet all our needs. God will not allow it. He created within us needs that He and He alone can meet. If we don't allow God to meet these needs for us, we will never be satisfied with the person we marry. When we allow God to meet our needs, we can say to our spouse, "I am not here because I have needs. I am here because I love you. I am strong in the Lord, and I have something to contribute to your life." Approaching a relationship with this attitude should be the goal of every Christian. Every principle laid out in this chapter is designed to ultimately lead us into a relationship where this attitude prevails. And when we enter into a relationship in this manner, it will be fulfilling and lasting.

↙ Chapter Twelve

A DATING PROGRESSION

Given all we discussed in the previous chapter, once we decide we're romantically attracted to someone, how should we progress to minimize potential hurt in the relationship and avoid the temptation to sin?

BE HONEST: ADMIT TO YOURSELF YOU FEEL ROMANTIC ATTRACTION FOR THE PERSON

Christians are notorious liars in this regard. "Oh, no," we say, "there is nothing here. We're just friends in the Lord." Yet while we're saying this, we are rearranging our whole schedule to be near the person, and we think about the person so much we keep tripping over the furniture and bumping into things!

It's not hard to identify whether we have feelings for another person. All we have to do is simply ask ourselves this question: "How would I feel if I learned this person was engaged to be married to someone else? Would it hurt?" If the answer is yes, then we're romantically attracted to that person. Sometimes people don't want to admit this to themselves because they don't want to get hurt, but in the end it is more hurtful not to be honest with ourselves.

We should admit this to ourselves at the very beginning of the relationship. In so doing, if the relationship is not right, it's easy to disentangle ourselves at this early stage. If we don't admit our romantic attraction right at the start, we can easily get into a relationship way over our head.

GOD IS FOR US. HE WANTS TO GIVE US THE VERY BEST.

SEEK THE LORD

Why is it so important to seek the Lord? Because we need to ask Him if we can progress. Remember, God is for us. He wants to give us the very best. If we don't ask the Lord how we should proceed, we might end up settling for second best in our life. God does not want us to do this, but all too often we get it turned around the wrong way. We think, "I know God is not really for me, and I know He is not into romantic relationships. I know what I want, and I'm mature enough to make up my own mind. I won't ask God about this right now. I'll wait until we're in love, and then I'll ask God what He thinks, and He'll be so impressed with how much we love each other that He will say it's okay to get married." But this is pure and simple manipulation, not to mention self-deception.

SEEKING THE LORD IN A RELATIONSHIP IS NOT A ONE-TIME EVENT.

Young people come to me and say, "We have been seeking the Lord about our relationship, and we have been praying, and we can't get a clear answer." I say to them, "Do you know why you can't get a clear answer? It's because God is not talking to you. You don't want to hear what God has to say. You've been manipulating Him into saying what you want to hear, and He won't say it. You have backed God into a corner, giving Him only two options. Either He goes along with your choice, or He crushes you. You won't hear from Him again until you repent and put your relationship on the altar and tell Him you are willing to do whatever He says."

Seeking the Lord in a relationship is not a one-time event. Sure, we may have prayed about it six months ago and God showed us it was fine to keep seeing each other. But we need His direction as we proceed in the relationship. We need to involve the Lord in our relationship every step of the way. We need to be asking Him if we're still on track. This kind of humility brings God into a relationship. Remember, Satan will do whatever he can to (a) promote a relationship that is not God's highest for us or (b) mess up a relationship that is God's highest for us. Either way, we need to stay close to God. As we proceed in a relationship, yellow lights should be flashing, reminding us to proceed with extreme caution.

> It is a trap for a man to dedicate something rashly and only later to consider his vows. (Proverbs 20:25)

MAKE JESUS LORD OF YOUR EMOTIONS

Don't be an emotional prostitute. What is a prostitute? A prostitute is someone who is willing to have sex with anyone who is willing to pay for it. Money is a prostitute's only criterion. You don't see prostitutes wearing billboards that say things like, "Will sleep with tall blond. Sun-tanned with Southern accent only." No, all they care about is that the person has the money to pay. So what is an emotional prostitute? An emotional prostitute is a person who's willing to date anyone who will pay him or her a little attention. The person's emotions are out there for the taking. It doesn't matter whether the other person is a Christian or not, or whether he or she is emotionally whole or not. All that matters is that the person gets paid with attention.

All of us who are Christians need to make a pact with the Lord and promise Him that we are not going to allow anyone to have an emotional bond with us unless He says it is okay. God is more interested in us than anyone else is. If we commit our emotions to Him, He will keep them safe.

> My son, give me your heart and let your eyes keep to my ways. (Proverbs 23:26)

SUBMIT AND COMMUNICATE YOUR RELATIONSHIP TO AN OBJECTIVE PERSON

Love is a heady thing. It is impossible to keep our perspective when we're in love, no matter how hard we try. That is why we need an objective third party to help us. This person needs to be someone who knows us well and is committed to our well-being. It could be a parent or a pastor, but whoever it is, it needs to be a person who is not emotionally involved. Our best friend is probably not the right person to ask, since our friend is likely to say, "Wow, go for it!" Nor is our mother the right person if she thinks no one will ever be good enough for us.

Age has nothing to do with our need for an objective person. I have counseled people in their thirties and forties who have lost all sense of objectivity. They are head over heels in love with someone while everyone around them is shaking their heads and pointing out that it will never work. We all need another pair of eyes to watch out for us.

When I met my wife, Michelle, I was twenty-eight years old. I was a youth pastor and had counseled people who were single and people who were married, but now everything was different. It was not theory anymore. My emotions were involved, and I needed to talk things out with someone I could trust. I chose a friend I knew would tell things to me straight. There were issues that came up as Michelle and I dated, and I'm sure that if I had not had my friend to help me see things and get me over some obstacles, I would not have been able to make a marriage commitment to Michelle.

All of us need counsel and guidance. Most of all, we need this counsel and guidance when we're in the throes of an important relationship.

The way of a fool seems right to him, but a wise man listens to advice. (Proverbs 12:15)

TODAY WE SEEM TO HAVE TOTALLY LOST THE ART OF WAITING FOR SOMEONE WE LOVE.

COMMUNICATE WITH YOUR PARTNER

Up until this point we have not done anything to alert the other person to the fact that we are romantically interested in him or her. Once we initially have the green light on the first four points—that is, we have been honest with ourselves and sought God's direction while affirming Jesus as Lord of our emotions and submitting our intentions to an objective person—we need to find the right timing to communicate how we feel to the person we are attracted to. But we must undertake this communication in the most loving way. For example, if a man and a woman are going on an overseas outreach together, it may not be the most loving time for the man to tell the woman how he feels about her just as they are leaving the church parking lot. Why not? Because what if the woman doesn't know how to react? What if she needs time to think the whole thing through, just as the man did? If this is the case, his words could make the whole outreach unnecessarily awkward. The couple would be bumping into each other all the time. And what if she does respond positively to the announcement of his feelings for her? The entire outreach could go by in a flood of romantic feelings and hormones, with neither of them being of any use to God's work at all. It would be much better for the man to wait until they get back from the outreach where the two of them have the time and circumstances to pursue a relationship.

Today we seem to have totally lost the art of waiting for someone we love. When I read biographies of missionaries from the last century, I'm struck by how they waited for God's timing. Often they were engaged for years and separated by continents, yet they did not complain. We're such a *now* generation. We think we have a right to whatever makes us happy immediately. And being this way, we will never know how many of God's blessings we have missed out on.

WE MUST ALWAYS ALLOW THE OTHER PERSON A GRACIOUS WAY OUT. IT'S THE LOVING THING TO DO.

When we communicate with the other person we need to do it wisely and unselfishly. Again, we need to think of the most loving way to communicate how we feel. Don't shock the other person. Remember, we have had time to think things over, but the other person may have no idea we're interested in him or her. The other person might not feel the same way about a relationship as we do. Don't go up to a person and say, "I want you to know I really like you and would like to have three kids with you. Is that okay with you?" Such an approach is simply a manipulative shock tactic. Emotional blackmail is another manipulative shock tactic. "I'm in love with you, and if you don't feel the same way about me, my life will be ruined. I might even commit suicide. So how about a date tomorrow night?" None of us, I hope, would ever be this blatant, but I think you get the idea of the wrong way to communicate how you feel. And when we share, we must always allow the other person a gracious way out. It's the loving thing to do. If we follow this pattern and the other person does enter into a relationship with us, we will have the security of knowing that our feelings are being reciprocated freely and that the other person has not been manipulated and trapped into doing something he or she doesn't want to do.

Once we begin to communicate our feelings, we must continue to communicate. At every stage in a relationship, we need to be sure that we are verbally communicating what we're thinking and that the other person is as committed to the next step in the relationship as we are. This process goes something like this: I tell the other person I like her and wait for her reply. If she says she likes me, then I ask her if she would like to go out with me. And if she would, we go out together. We date for a while, and then I tell the person I *really* like her and have never liked another person as much. Then I wait. If she says she feels the same way without feeling any pressure or manipulation from me, then I can proceed with the relationship.

WE MUST BE CAREFUL TO NEVER COMMIT OUR EMOTIONS BEYOND THE POINT WHERE OUR PARTNER HAS STATED HIS OR HER EMOTIONS ARE.

We must be careful to never commit our emotions beyond the point where our partner has stated his or her emotions are. We must never allow ourselves to get into a position where we are flipped out over someone and have no idea how the person feels about us. Rather, we should check that the other person matches us emotion for emotion, and if he or she doesn't, then we should back off and give the person time. We should also be prepared to let the relationship die. It is much more loving to do this than to press on regardless. If we are not careful, we can end up married for the wrong reason. A tenderhearted person can think, "Look how much she needs me. Look how much I'm helping! She says she has never felt closer to Jesus than when we are together." Even though this person does not have the same feelings as the other partner in the relationship, the couple continues on because of manipulation or a sense of being needed or a sense of guilt. People often commit to marry someone they're not really in love with because the other person needs them so much. A marriage like this is not a loving act on the part of either party. If one person is forceful enough to override the uncertainty of another, it will come back to haunt them both, and they will have to deal with it later on in the marriage. The person who feels emotionally trapped into marrying someone will have a lifetime to reflect on what the other person did to him or her and to resent that person for it. Everyone deserves better than that.

DETERMINE TO PLEASE GOD

A Christian does not please God when he or she becomes romantically involved with an unsaved person. When our emotions get in the way and we start to fall in love, we begin to rationalize the situation. Eventually we lose our perspective and can even end up married to a non-Christian. The apostle Paul tells us we shouldn't be mismatched with unbelievers. Such a partnership, he points out, is unrighteous. Light and darkness cannot fellowship together (1 Corinthian 6:14).

When young people read this verse, the girls often say, "Yeah, all the hot guys are non-Christians. If I date only Christian guys, I'll end up married to a nerd." The boys say, "There sure are some babes out there. Am I really stuck with the girls in Sunday school?" When we think like this, we're implying that God can't lead us to the most attractive, most sexy, most wonderful person who is just perfect for us. We're implying that God will pull someone from the reject bin and ask us to take him or her. But we know that's simply not true.

The reason a Christian is not to marry a non-Christian has to do with submission. In Ephesians chapter five, Paul gives us the blueprint for a Christian family. He says to both husbands and wives, "Be subject [or submitted] to one another out of reverence to Christ." How can we as Christian men and women allow ourselves to get into a marriage where the Bible tells us to submit to Christ and also to submit to a non-Christian spouse? It will not work because it is inevitable that the two "submissions" will conflict, causing us to make a choice. I have seen more Christian married people faced with this choice than I care to remember. Many of them have spent their lives trying to resolve their loyalty to God and their loyalty to their spouse's wishes. God never intended His children to live with this kind of stress. So we need to do ourselves a favor and not put ourselves in a situation where we might fall in love with someone who has not made Jesus his or her Lord and Savior. Satan loves it when this happens because it means he has successfully sabotaged another prospective Christian family, and functional Christian families are a tremendous witness for Christ.

CONCLUSION

The creation of a functional Christian family is the ultimate end for a romantic relationship. It is where all the principles laid out in this book lead. God created us not for isolation but for fellowship: fellowship with Him and with other human beings. We started this book by examining God's bottom line for all relationships, that we first and foremost love Him and then that we love others, our neighbors, as we would want to be loved and treated. From there we went on to discover some important principles that will guide us in developing a romantic relationship with a member of the opposite sex.

As we come to the end of this book, I encourage you to reread these principles until they are etched into your mind. By doing so, and then following the principles, you will save yourself tremendous potential heartache and pain while allowing the Lord to lead you into a relationship that is the most committed, meaningful, and fulfilling relationship possible.

Of course, there may be some of you who are saying to yourselves, "Hold it. I've totally blown it. I've broken just about every principle you've laid out here. There's no hope for me. I've messed things up big-time." Well, I have good news for you: There is no mess so big that God cannot clean it up. God is in the business of redemption. He delights in giving people new starts. So don't despair. There is hope. Read the next chapter, "What If I Have Already Blown It?" In it you will find practical steps you can take to get your life and your relationships back in order and under the Lordship of Jesus.

Chapter Thirteen

WHAT IF I HAVE ALREADY BLOWN IT?

Some of you who have read this book may find yourselves thinking, "I've blown it! I have already messed things up badly. I have dated for all the wrong reasons. I've allowed myself to fall in love with the wrong person. I've slept around." For some, the list may go on and on. These are serious issues, but I have good news. God is in the business of redemption! If you take the following seven steps, God has promised to restore you and to set your feet back on the path to life and healthy, meaningful relationships.

> As far as the east is from the west, so far has he removed our transgressions from us. (Psalm 103:12)

Think about this for a moment. Meditate on how far the east is from the west, and realize that's how far God is willing and able to remove our sins from us. That is good news indeed!

STEP ONE: REPENT BEFORE GOD

God will not forgive the things we do not repent of. If we justify our actions by saying, "I'm really no worse than a lot of other people, and better than some," or "I had a poor role model grow-ing up, so I can't be held responsible," we will never be forgiven. We need to read back over the list of words and their meanings in chapter nine and ask God to convict us of our sin. Then we must denounce it and repent.

GOD WILL NOT FORGIVE THE THINGS WE DO NOT REPENT OF.

STEP TWO: MAKE APPROPRIATE RESTITUTION TO THE PEOPLE YOU HAVE HURT

If you have hurt someone else, apologize and make things right with the person if it is appropriate. How do you know what is appropriate? Use the same litmus test that has been applied consistently throughout this book. Ask yourself, "Is this the most loving thing I could do for this person at this time?" Sometimes the answer will be no. It is neither wise nor loving to write a let-ter to someone else's wife to apologize for a sexual relationship you had with her before she was married. It might, however, be appropriate to apologize to the person you're dating right now and whom you don't particularly like but are dating because you have been so insecure you had to play the dating game. If it is wise and loving, then do it. But it generally isn't wise or loving to write to someone else's wife or husband.

STEP THREE: VERBALLY RENOUNCE ANY SEXUAL RELATIONSHIPS YOU HAVE HAD OUTSIDE OF MARRIAGE

Go someplace where you can be alone and verbally sever the link that sex has formed between you and the person you were involved with. Tell Satan he can no longer control your memo-ries and emotions towards that person. Tell him you have repented and God has cleansed you from all unrighteousness.

STEP FOUR: FORGIVE PEOPLE WHO HAVE FAILED YOU

Whoever these people are or wherever they may be, forgive them. Think of the words of the Lord's prayer: "Give us today our daily bread. Forgive us our debts, as we also have forgiven our debtors." Forgive people who have failed you, forgive your parents, and forgive yourself.

STEP FIVE: WALK IN THE FORGIVENESS AND CLEANSING GOD GIVES YOU

What does this mean? Basically it means we must continually acknowledge and accept the work Jesus did for us on the cross.

> If we claim to be without sin, we deceive ourselves and the truth is not in us. If we confess our sins, he is faithful and just and will forgive us our sins and purify us from all unrighteousness. (1 John 1:8–9)

If God forgives us, we must forgive ourselves. One of the descriptions of Satan is the "accuser of the brethren." In Revelation we read:

> Then I heard a loud voice in heaven say: "Now have come the salvation and the power of the kingdom of our God, and the authority of his Christ. For the accuser of our brothers, who accuses them before our God day and night, has been hurled down. They overcame him by the blood of the Lamb and by the word of their testimony..." (Revelation 12:10–11)

THE BLOOD OF JESUS CHRIST
HAS CLEANSED US FROM *ALL* SIN.

Satan will always throw our past at us if we let him. But we don't have to. The blood of Jesus Christ has cleansed us from *all* sin. That means even the worst sexual sin we could have committed. We must never accept Satan's lie that we are used goods or that what we have done is too bad to be forgiven. Resist guilt and condemnation. We are acceptable as a bride of Christ, pure and holy in God's sight. We are forgiven and cleansed, and we need to remind ourselves and Satan of this fact as many times a day as it takes for us to be convinced of it.

STEP SIX: DEVELOP HEALING IN YOUR LIFE

Often wounds caused by relationships are tender for a long time afterwards. So we must cultivate an attitude of healing in our lives. When a hurtful memory assaults us, we should say, "Thank You, Jesus. You are healing me from this hurt. I am trusting You to turn it into a memory that does not hurt me anymore."

STEP SEVEN: THANK GOD

Whatever state you find yourself in, thank God that He wants to restore you to wholeness. He wants to restore your ability to enjoy intimacy with Him and with others. The same God who created you can restore you. God can put you back together and lead you into healthy, whole, and fulfilling relationships, and that, after all, is what Christianity is all about.

↙ Study Guide

FOR INDIVIDUALS AND GROUPS

↳ Study Questions

---

1) WORLD, WE HAVE A PROBLEM

Personal Study Questions ─────────────────────

1. How much of your time/emotional energy goes into thinking about romantic and/or sexual relationships, real or imagined?

2. What kind of emotional impact have romantic and/or sexual relationships had in your life so far?

3. In what ways have you been affected by other people's relationship problems?

4. How much of a "light set on a hilltop" do you think you are in the area of relationships?

Group Discussion

1. How well does your local fellowship address the needs and concerns of people with regard to their questions about relationships? Explain why you think this way.

2. What are some of the media messages we are bombarded with regarding romantic and sexual relationships? Give some specific examples.

3. In what ways do these media messages conflict with our Christian values?

4. Do you think Christian young people react significantly different than non-Christians to these media messages?

5. On a scale of 1–10, how interested do you think God is in human relationships? Why?

6. Could your group be described as a "light set on a hilltop" with regard to romantic/sexual relationships?

7. Do you think avoiding the entire topic is a viable way of dealing with the issue? Why or why not?

∼ Study Questions

---

2) THE BOTTOM LINE

Personal Study Questions ————————————————

1. Which is most difficult for you personally: to love God, to love yourself, or to love others? Why?

2. Do you think you tend towards humanistic or mystic thinking? What specific verses can you use to stay balanced in this area?

3. List three problems you face or have faced in your life. To what degree and in what way were they related to a breakdown in relationships?

4. Is there one person or group of people you need to relate to in a better way? Who are they?

5. Think of an effective form of witnessing you have been involved in or heard about. How tied to relationship building was it? If it was tied to relationship building, why was this important?

6. If a non-Christian looked closely at your relationships, would this person be attracted to Jesus or repelled by what he or she saw?

7. Are there specific instances in your life where you need to repent of pride in a particular relationship and ask God for wisdom and humility?

8. Do you have inferior pride that stops you from doing all God has called you to do?

9. If origin and purpose give something its value, what is your origin and what is your purpose? How much value does this give you?

Group Discussion

1. Why is God worthy of our love? What are some ways in which we can demonstrate our love for Him?

2. Do you know people who equate God with loving feelings? How could you help them to see the error of their thinking?

3. How can we convince people that not all religious roads lead to God?

4. What are some relationship issues facing your community? How are these related to pride?

5. How open is your church to accepting members with different gifts and abilities? Could you improve on this? How?

6. In the illustrations of the 100-dollar bill and the cockroach, what is the point? How can this be translated into personal actions?

Study Questions

---

3) BACK TO THE BEGINNING

Personal Study Questions ————————————————

1. What are some of the pleasures God has given you to enjoy? Have you thanked Him for them lately?

2. Have you struggled with the idea that God made your body and its potential for sexual pleasure? If so, in what way have you struggled?

3. Have you ever blamed outward images or objects for your lust? Why is this a cop-out? Are you prepared to take responsibility for your own sins in this regard?

4. What are some of the messages Satan has tried to deceive you with regarding sex and relationships?

Group Discussion

1. What are some examples of God's creativity we see around us?

2. In what obvious ways do Christians try to distance religion and sexuality?

3. Who are some of the people the non-Christian world portrays as role models in the area of relationships? In what ways are they good or bad role models?

4. Who do you think is a good role model in the area of relationships? Why?

Study Questions

4) TWISTED TRUTHS

Personal Study Questions ——————————————

1. Are there some things about your body or personality that have made you feel different from other people or as if you don't fit in?

2. Have there been situations in your life where feeling different has led you to feel inferior to others?

3. Read Psalm 139:13–14 aloud to yourself. Can you agree with what it says about the way God made you?

4. In what way have you compared yourself to others? The Bible tells us this is not wise. Why do you think it says that?

5. Identify two or three popular media images that falsely define what is supposedly masculine or feminine. What is the goal of their designers? How does the false definition impact you?

Group Discussion

1. What are some cultural norms we confuse with the fundamentals of being male or female?

2. How can we begin to see our uniqueness as an asset and not a liability? How can we encourage each other to be who we really are?

3. Name some role models who are definitely unique but also good witnesses for Christ.

4. Identify and discuss two popular media images that falsely define what is supposedly masculine.

5. Identify and discuss two popular media images that falsely define what is supposedly feminine.

Study Questions

5) The Gift of Attraction

Personal Study Questions ————————————————

1. Have you seen your attraction gift as a blessing or a problem? When and why?

2. What kind of people, male and female, do you personally feel attracted to?

3. Are you able to turn your attraction gift on and off at will? Why or why not?

4. What is the difference between feeling an attraction towards someone and acting on that feeling?

5. Have there been times in your life where you have acted on attractions that were inappropriate for some reason?

6. Is it acceptable to leave room for a little lust in your life? What measures can you take to prevent lust?

7. Do you have a balanced view of a person's internal and external qualities, or do you think you're too preoccupied with what a person looks like on the outside? If you have an unbalanced view, what has this imbalance led to or could it lead to?

Group Discussion

1. As a group, do you provide enough opportunities for members of the opposite sex to get to know each other well? Could you do better, and if so, how?

2. Is your fellowship or small group a place where you can meet with members of the opposite sex in a way that does not attract teasing or speculation from others?

3. As a group are you too quick to assign "boyfriend" and "girlfriend" status to people, making it more difficult for them to explore a wide range of relationships?

4. Do you feel there is a pressure on you to pair off? What can be done to lessen this pressure?

5. Do you think it's okay for girls or guys to do all they can to make themselves look attractive to the opposite sex? Why or why not?

6. What should you tell a person who blames his or her problem with lust on the way someone else behaves?

7. In what way is lust related to how we value other human beings?

.᠘ Study Questions

---

6) THE ROMANTIC GIFT

Personal Study Questions ————————————————

1. Have you fallen prey to the idea that falling in love is outside your control? Why is this a false idea, and how does acknowledging that you are in control of your attraction gift change the way you live your life?

2. What goals do you have that you believe God wants you to meet before falling in love?

3. What are some criteria or traits a person would have or meet before you allowed yourself to fall in love with him or her?

4. How might you tell whether you are driven by your romantic gift or controlling it? If you are driven by it, how can you reverse this?

Group Discussion

1. Why don't you have to be in love with someone else?

2. Name some instances where it would be inappropriate for you to be in love with someone else.

3. Why do you think God put us in control of our attraction gift and not vice versa?

4. What advice would you give a married person who said he or she had "fallen out of love" with his or her spouse?

5. What are some of the consequences to other people when a person does not take control of his or her attraction gift?

6. What role should feelings play in any commitment you have made, whether it is to God or to a spouse? Are feelings important?

⊱ Study Questions

7) LOGICAL AND LOVING LIMITS

Personal Study Questions ─────────────────────

1. What are some gifts God has given you that you can use in a constructive or a destructive way?

2. What kind of reasons have you been given for Christians not having sex outside of marriage?

3. For you, are the above reasons a strong enough basis for rejecting sex outside of marriage?

4. Are there some areas of your life, including your sexuality, that have mastery over you right now?

5. In thinking about the Corinthian Christians, which view do you tend towards: the avoid-relationships-with-the-opposite-sex-altogether view or Greek dualism?

6. Have you involved yourself in sexual activities that were outside of God's best for you? Have you repented and asked God to help you in the future?

Group Discussion

1. What are the common reasons given for a Christian not to have sex outside of marriage? Do those reasons make sense to you? Do they need to?

2. In the passage 1 Corinthians 6:12–20, what is Paul saying about the way in which sexual sin is different from any other sin?

3. Do you think this view of sexual relationships also holds true for non-Christians? Why or why not?

4. In television shows that depict casual sex, what are some of the consequences of these sexual encounters? In real life, what are some of the results of casual sex?

5. How would you respond to the statement, "Hey, I wouldn't want to buy a new car without taking it for a test drive?"

✒ Study Questions

---

8) DAMAGE DONE

Personal Study Questions ———————————

1. What are some of the ways you would be damaged if you had sexual relations outside of marriage?

2. Have you seen those consequences in your life or in the lives of people around you?

3. Do you think it's important to be committed to someone and have an assurance of his or her commitment through marriage before becoming sexually involved? Why or why not?

4. How has your life been affected by your own or other people's inappropriate sexual activities? Are you able to forgive those who have sinned against you in this way?

5. Reflecting on the river analogy, do you consider your sexuality to be a deep calm river running within its banks or a raging flood destroying things in its path?

6. Do you know someone who can either help you to rebuild the banks or encourage you to stay within them when faced with temptation?

Group Discussion

1. What are some of the things that can be used to lower your resistance to sexual encounters? Why are they effective?

2. Why is marriage the only commitment deep enough to bond two people for life?

3. In our culture, what are some of the other ways we formalize commitments in business, personal, and family matters? Why are these important?

4. Should Christian leaders give information to single people in the church about AIDS and condom use? Why or why not?

5. What are some of the destructive results you have noticed as a result of sex outside of the marriage commitment?

6. What is so wrong with having sex with someone you know you are going to marry anyway? Is it that bad?

7. What can an unmarried person do now that will help him or her have a trusting and open relationship in marriage with regard to sexual matters?

✎ Study Questions

---

9) HOW FAR IS TOO FAR?

Personal Study Questions

1. Thinking back over the way you have behaved in previous relationships, did your behavior pass the test of "Is it right? Is it loving? Is it wise?" Does your behavior in your relationships today pass the test?

2. What are some of the ways in which you could stir up or have stirred up inappropriate responses in another person?

3. Why is it appealing to let yourself go sometimes? What are the results of following through with this behavior?

4. Are you driven by the desire to have a girlfriend or boyfriend at all times? If so, why?

5. Why is it so important for you to work out your views on what is appropriate on a date before you ever go on one? What is likely to happen if you don't do this?

6. Have you ever used a member of the opposite sex to get what you wanted? If so, what was it you wanted? Was it wrong to do this?

7. Have you ever committed spiritual adultery against God? How is this linked to the idea of adultery in a marriage? What are the similarities?

8. How can you focus on the long-term goal of a faithful, committed relationship over the quick "buzz" of sexual sins? What is your biggest obstacle here, and how can you plot a course around it?

Group Discussion

1. List some of the things you consider appropriate or inappropriate on a date. Where did you get the list from? Are you able to keep to it?

2. What do the media portray as appropriate for single dating couples? How can we counteract the messages being aimed at us every day?

3. If everything is permissible for a Christian, what is to stop him or her from doing all types of sinful things?

4. Why are internal constraints far more effective in our society than external ones? If all the laws in our country were revoked, would there be chaos? Would you participate in it? Why or why not?

5. How can you tell whether a person is preoccupied with sexual or romantic thoughts? In what ways could you approach that person to help him or her?

6. How does society, and even our family and friends, encourage us to believe that we need to have a boyfriend or girlfriend at all times? How can we reverse this trend?

7. How would you respond to a person who said that pornography was a victimless crime and should not be regulated?

8. What kind of date would you say fits the category "dating for the glory of God"? Is this really realistic? What would be necessary to make it a reality in your dating experience?

⁓ Study Questions

10) WALLS OF PROTECTION

Personal Study Questions ———————————————

1. Are you able to trust God to lead you to the right partner for you at the right time? What is the most difficult part of doing this?

2. To what extent has your family life mirrored the biblical ideal of parents loving God, loving each other, and loving their children? Are you willing to forgive any shortcomings your parents have had in meeting these ideals?

3. Have you ever been rebellious toward your parents or others in authority over you? Has this coincided with doing harmful things to yourself? Why did you allow yourself to do those things?

4. What role can neglect play in a family? What steps could be taken to repair the damage done by neglect?

Group Discussion

1. What conclusions can be drawn from the story of Rebekah and Isaac? Which aspects of their story are useful to us today?

2. How can you stay submitted to your parents while away at college or living on your own? When would it be inappropriate for you to be submitted to them? What should you do in that instance?

3. Thinking back over the news of the past month, what are some of the consequences for a family in which the walls of protection have been broken down?

4. Who is ultimately responsible when a marriage breaks apart? Why?

5. What would you say to a non-Christian who did not care whether he or she had sex that resulted in AIDS or a pregnancy? How could you help the person to see or to care that he or she is destroying himself or herself?

6. What role do you believe mutual submission between a husband and wife plays in forming the protective wall around a family? What act is the opposite of submission? How would this opposite act damage the protective wall?

✑ Study Questions

---

11) A DATING PHILOSOPHY

Personal Study Questions ————————————

1. Have you had a dating philosophy in the past? If so, what was it? Are there some things you now think you need to change? If so, what?

2. What kinds of things are chords that bind you romantically to another person?

3. Have you ever experienced the pain of a relationship where your emotions have been left dangling? How did that happen? How can you prevent it from happening again (or at least lessen the impact of it)?

4. When have you dated a person for the wrong motive? What was the result?

5. Where and when can you meet datable people who share the same dating philosophy as you do?

6. In what ways can you show your date that you value him or her as a person created by God for fellowship with Him?

7. What are some ways you can be sure you know the whole person you are dating rather than just a projected image?

8. What could you be doing now that would make you attractive to the type of partner you would like in the future?

9. In the past, have you seen the need for sex in the same category as the need for air or food? Why is this perception false?

Group Discussion

1. List some alternate dating philosophies. Which ones have you used in the past? Which ones do you use at present?

2. Why do you think a romantic breakup is so difficult? Do you think it hurts a guy or a girl more? Give reasons for your answer.

3. What kinds of actions/activities bind us romantically to our partner? How are they interpreted differently by guys and girls? How should this affect our actions in dating?

4. Who is more responsible to follow through on a dating philosophy, a guy or a girl? Why do you say that? Can you back it up biblically?

5. What are some of the results of dating someone for the wrong motives that you've observed?

6. Do you think your church provides enough ways for people to meet with members of the opposite sex in a nonromantic setting? How could it do better? Are there some activities that focus people on romantic relationships in an unhealthy way? What are they, and how can they be made to reflect a more healthy view of relationships?

7. What would you say to a non-Christian friend who calls you a prude for not wanting to have sex before marriage?

Study Questions

---

12) A DATING PROGRESSION

Personal Study Questions ————————————————

1. Do you have a romantic attraction towards another person? Is it easy to admit to yourself? Why or why not?

2. What should you do if you have a romantic attraction towards someone that is inappropriate?

3. How can you be sure you constantly put God first in any relationship? What might happen if you don't?

4. Are you an emotional prostitute? In what way? How can you stop having your emotions out there for sale?

5. If you were to get (or are) involved in a romantic relationship, whom would you submit your actions to? Why would you choose this person?

6. How can you prevent yourself from reading things into a relationship that may not be actually there?

7. Is your bottom line to please God in all you do? How will that translate into how you conduct yourself in a romantic relationship?

Group Discussion

1. Why should you seek the Lord sooner rather than later in a relationship?

2. With whom would it be inappropriate to pursue a romantic relationship? What should you do if you feel a romantic attraction towards someone like that? Should you tell the person?

3. In what ways do Christians and non-Christians approach dating differently?

4. What are some factors that make it difficult to communicate honestly with a date? How can these factors be overcome, and why is it so important that they are?

5. What is the result of manipulating a person into a long-term relationship or marriage with you? Is it worth it in the long run?

6. Do you agree with this statement: In a marriage it is important that both parties are attracted to each other physically, emotionally, and spiritually. Why or why not?

13) WHAT IF I HAVE ALREADY BLOWN IT?

Personal and Group Study Questions ─────────────

1. Meditate on Psalm 103:12. What does this verse mean to you? What impact can the truth of this Psalm have in a believer's restoration process?

2. What key truth should guide us when considering how best to make restitution to someone we have hurt? What part does confidentiality play when making restitution to someone from our past?

3. Why is forgiving whose who failed us so important to our personal restoration?

4. What does it mean to "walk in forgiveness"? How does dwelling on past failure affect our life in Christ?

5. What role does thankfulness play in our restoration? What is the opposite of thankfulness? How might dwelling on this "opposite" impact our Christian walk?

LIFE-CHANGING BOOKS, CASSETTES, AND VIDEOS FROM DEAN SHERMAN

Spiritual Warfare for Every Christian
Includes study guide (paper, 210 pages) $11.99

Spiritual Warfare Audio Set
12 cassettes $39.99

Spiritual Warfare Video Set
12 videos $120.00

Love, Sex, and Relationships
Includes study guide (paper, 208 pages) $11.99

Relationships Audio Set
6 cassettes $24.99

Relationships Video Set
8 videos $80.00

Balance Audio Set
6 cassettes $19.99

For these and other quality materials from YWAM Publishing, visit your local Christian bookstore or call 1-800-922-2143 for a free catalog of materials.